CAJUN COOKING

Succulent Recipes From Louisiana

CAJUN COOKING

Succulent Recipes From Louisiana

MARJIE LAMBERT

HACKBERRY PRESS

TO TERRY
who offered me diamonds, adventure,
and inspiration.

A QUANTUM BOOK

Published by
Hackberry Press, a division of The Texas Bookman
2700 Lone Star Drive
Dallas
Texas 75212
USA

Copyright ©MCMXCIII
Quintet Publishing Ltd.

This edition printed 2003

ISBN 1-931040-31-1

QUMCAJ

This book is produced by
Quantum Publishing Ltd
6 Blundell Street
London N7 9BH

Printed in Singapore by
Star Standard Industries (Pte) Ltd.

AUTHOR'S ACKNOWLEDGEMENTS
With special thanks to my dad, who taught me not to be afraid of
experimenting, and Elaine Corn, who helped me turn my experiments
into recipes. Thanks also to Judith and Lindsay at Quintet and to Bob
Townsend and Zoe Zahner at Dingus McGee's.

PICTURE CREDITS
The Publisher would like to thank the following for the supply of
additional photographic material used in this book.

Key: *t* = top; *b* = bottom; *l* = left; *r* = right.
Michael Freeman: pages 9, 11, 66 *tl tr bl*, 67, 109.
Louisiana Office of Tourism: pages 6, 7, 10, 12, 22, 27, 34, 42, 44, 50,
66 *br*, 84 *l r,* 88, 106

CONTENTS

INTRODUCTION

— ★ —

Louisiana cooking is a great conglomeration of influences from the many ethnic groups that have populated the state for more than 200 years. Yet, each ingredient in that melting pot is distinct and can be traced to its roots.

In Louisiana, and especially in New Orleans, life frequently revolves around food and discussions of food. There is a great love of food and cooking that predated and outlasted America's brief 1980s' love affair with celebrity chefs and the chic restaurant of the moment. Many of New Orleans' best restaurants are known far beyond Louisiana and have been operating for several decades, oddities in an industry known for short-lived ventures.

It is a telling piece of evidence that when Cajuns trace their history from Nova Scotia to Louisiana, it is intertwined with a story about food. It goes like this:

In 1755, when British soldiers drove a colony of French settlers out of Nova Scotia and their colony of Acadia for refusing to swear allegiance to Britain, the lobster went with the Acadians, according to the legend. The Acadians and the lobster, the legend continues, wandered for years through Canada and the east coast colonies of what would become the United States, until they reached Louisiana, colonized by the French nearly a century earlier. Finding kinship there, and swampy land that no one else wanted, the Acadians settled along the waterways of southern Louisiana, south and west of New Orleans. The name Acadians, through years of mispronounciation, was eventually shortened to Cajuns. And the lobster, worn down to a tiny creature by the long, hard trip, settled into the bayous and became the crawfish.

The crawfish, Louisiana's most valuable commercial catch, is still one of the Cajun's best friends. It is a staple – and often the unofficial logo – of Cajun cooking, a style of cuisine that is based on the country French cooking of their ancestors, but evolves around local ingredients and a distinctive way of cooking. Gumbo uses many of the same ingredients as French bouillabaisse, for example, but the Cajun methods of preparation disguise those bloodlines.

The staples of Cajun food were what the Cajuns could hunt, catch, or grow. From the bayous, they pulled crawfish, alligators, frogs, and dozens of species of fish. The coastal marshes were – and still are – a midway point for ducks and other game birds that migrate each year between Canada and South America, and a winter home for some ducks. From the Gulf of Mexico, the Cajuns caught shrimp and oyster and more fish. They grew large home gardens – especially sweet potatoes, Creole tomatoes, squashes, eggplants, and, of course, okra – in the rich soil and subtropical climate, and raised chicken and pigs.

Creole cuisine is the more sophisticated city cousin of Cajun cooking. It also has French roots, but has been more influenced by the cooking of other ethnic groups. Louisiana, a French crown colony in the early 1700s, was ceded to Spain, then went back to French control before the United States bought it in the great Louisiana Purchase of 1803. There were large immigrations of Germans, Italians and Hungarians, while the slave trade brought thousands of Africans. Local Indians also contributed to the cuisine. New Orleans, being a port city, was a center for trade with the West Indies, Cuba and Mexico. Where Cajun cooking is hearty and rustic country fare, Creole-style food is more aristocratic. But in many cases, the line between the two cuisines has been blurred or erased.

In addition to local ingredients, Louisiana cuisine is typified by thick and complex sauces, the use of roux and freshly made stocks, and long cooking times. Seasoning is critical as well. Louisiana cooks say their dishes should have a flavor to set each taste bud off and keep it dancing. Most Cajun food is very spicy – it sometimes seems that you should just dump the entire contents of your spice rack into some dishes, but in reality the flavors are carefully chosen to complement each other and fill the mouth with sensation – and many are also hot with cayenne and other peppers. Many recipes begin with the Holy Trinity of Louisiana cooking: that is, chopped onions, bell peppers and celery.

Although Cajuns have been in southern Louisiana for more than two centuries, it was many years before their cooking began to spread beyond the bayous of what they called new Acadiana. Physically, the Cajuns remained fairly isolated until the mid 1970s, when the construction of an interstate highway across the wilderness of the Atchafalaya Basin created a shortcut between New Orleans and the

OPPOSITE Lafayette is the cultural heart of Acadiana. It boasts the Acadian Village, an historical re-creation of a Cajun community of the 1800s. Every spring, Lafayette celebrates the Azalea Trail, pictured here.

ABOVE Avery Island lies near New Iberia, deep in Cajun country. Its 300 acres are a horticultural paradise, thick with camellias, irises, azaleas and tropical plants, and a bird sanctuary where egrets nest.

heart of Cajun country. A few years later, Cajun cooking styles began to spread beyond New Orleans, and soon, the Cajun craze swept the United States.

For many people, their introduction to Cajun cooking was blackened redfish, a highly spiced fish fillet cooked very quickly at very high temperatures. Although not a traditional Cajun dish, it was an instant classic, and with good reason. But to many people, ignorant of a culinary history more than 200 years old, blackened redfish became the symbol of Cajun cooking. The demand created a shortage of redfish so severe that the state of Louisiana imposed a temporary ban on the sale of redfish caught in the Gulf of Mexico off Louisiana. Outside Louisiana, many people overlooked the gumbos, the jambalayas, the étouffées, and the crawfish – its history part of Cajun lore – and erroneously, and rather insultingly, defined Cajun cooking as simply anything blackened or anything seasoned with cayenne.

When Cajun fever subsided, and cooks stopped blackening everything from oysters to eggplant, it was clear that the recipes and ingredients of rural southern Louisiana cooks had influenced menus everywhere. Catfish became respectable. Andouille sausage, a spicy Cajun sausage of smoked pork, gained wide popularity – and imitators. Jambalaya was adopted by many cooks as part of their repertoire. So-called Cajun BBQ Shrimp – actually shrimp simmered in a butter sauce made incredibly hot by cayenne and other peppers – is hugely popular.

In some respects, Cajun cooking remains a style of another century. In an era of calorie and cholesterol consciousness, Cajun recipes use huge amounts of fat, butter and cream. There have been some concessions to health concerns, with Commander's Palace restaurant leading the way with lighter sauces, roux-less gumbos and traditional ingredients encased in light soufflés.

This cookbook tries to respond in the same way. It reduces the quantity of roux in many recipes, replaces heavy cream with light cream, cuts the amount of oil used to saute vegetables, and broils fish and sautes meat instead of deep-frying it where the taste of a dish is not significantly affected. But it is also true that heavy sauces and creams are integral to a style of cooking with a long history. Eliminate the roux, the cream soups and sauces, and the fried food and you eliminate the cuisine.

TRADITIONAL CAJUN INGREDIENTS

★

ABOVE *For more than two centuries, Cajun farmers have sold their luscious fruits and vegetables at over 100 produce stalls in the French Market in New Orleans' French Quarter.*

It's been said that the swamp floor is the pantry of the Cajun kitchen, and, indeed, the swamp produces one of the staples of the Cajun menu, the crawfish. Some of its other distinctive ingredients, including frogs, alligators and catfish, also come from the swamp. But the Gulf of Mexico gives Louisiana chefs their shrimp, oysters and dozens of varieties of fish. The Cajun hunting tradition contributes ducks, rabbits and other game animals. And the history of Cajuns in Louisiana, which dates back more than 200 years, is that of rural country folk relying on their gardens for produce and small farms for chicken and pork.

Most Cajun ingredients are widely available, they just are not displayed as prominently or in as great a quantity elsewhere as they are in Bayou country. The variety of crab or oyster in your grocery may be different than the type pulled from the waters of Louisiana, but all varieties work in the recipes in this book.

Widely used ingredients in Louisiana cooking include rice, which absorbs the rich sauces and tames the hot spices of Cajun dishes; cayenne and other hot peppers that are dried and ground and used for seasoning; Creole mustard, a sharp-tasting brown mustard with whole seeds; corn flour, a non-wheat flour milled from corn and used to bread items before frying; okra, a green pod vegetable that is sliced and used to thicken gumbo; filé powder, ground sassafras leaf that is used to season and thicken gumbo; mirliton, a pear-shaped vegetable related to the cucumber and also known as chayote; a wide variety of herbs, including parsley, thyme, oregano and basil; pecans; peaches; eggplants, green onions, artichokes, sweet potatoes, red beans, Creole tomatoes, and, of course, the Holy Trinity of bell peppers, onions and celery.

CRAWFISH. This creature, affectionately known as the mudbug because of its habit of tunneling deep into the mud to keep cool, has become a symbol of sorts for Cajun cooking. Although "crawdads" can be found on every continent except Africa, it is only in Cajun cooking that they have such an important part. Ninety percent of the world's commercial crawfish come from Louisiana, and most of those are eaten in Louisiana, although some are shipped around the world, especially to Finland and Sweden. With

OPPOSITE Paddleboats along the Mississippi River recall the 19th century, the days of Mark Twain and riverboat gamblers.

RIGHT Louisiana has miles and miles of rivers and swamps, and canoeing – alone or with a guide – can give a visitor a breathtaking sample of bayou country, including close-up views of alligators.

the growing popularity of Cajun cooking in the last decade, the demand for crawfish has increased to the point where people "farm" them commercially in ponds, which often double as rice paddies.

Louisiana's Cajun country is dotted with tiny places that serve boiled crawfish whole. They are one of the world's easiest meals. Throw some commercial crab and shrimp boil into boiling water in a big stockpot, add a sliced lemon and let simmer a few minutes to develop flavor, then add the live crawfish. Boil 10 minutes, drain and serve. To eat them, give the tail a quick twist until it snaps off from the rest of the body. Peel a couple of segments from the top of the tail, squeeze the tip, and the tail meat should pop out in one piece. Remove the black vein and eat.

Crawfish are generally available live, boiled whole and frozen, and in the form of tail meat that has been shelled and blanched. If your grocer or fish market does not carry crawfish, ask if they can special order it.

One of the newest items on the Cajun-Creole menu is the soft-shell crawfish, raised commercially in shallow trays and watched carefully until it sheds its shell. At this point it is plucked from the water and frozen before a new shell can harden.

The yellow-orange "fat" from the crawfish, actually its liver and pancreas, is considered a delicacy. Much of the wonderful flavor in a crawfish bisque comes from the fat.

CRAB. Blue-claw, soft-shell and buster crabs are the type most commonly used in Louisiana cuisine, but meat from other types of crab – Dungeness, King, Snow, and Stone crabs among others – work well in these recipes. Buying whole crabs is recommended, so the carcass can be used to make a delicious stock, but fresh, frozen and canned crab

meat are also available. In some places, crab claws, especially King Crab claws, are sold separately, pre-cooked and ready for dipping.

Soft-shell crabs are not a separate species of crab, but ones that are harvested in the brief period after they shed the shells they have outgrown, but before they grow new ones. Learn how much meat the whole crab available locally produces. It may take a dozen or more blue crabs to produce one pound of meat, but two medium Dungeness crabs will produce the same amount.

OYSTERS. Oysters are used generously in Cajun and Creole cooking. They are key ingredients in soups, gumbos and jambalayas, and are the stars of dishes such as Oysters Bienville (page 20–21) or Deep-Fried Oysters (page 22). Gulf Oysters and Louisiana Oysters are commonly used in Louisiana cooking, but use whatever fresh oysters are available locally. When buying oysters still in the shell, look for ones that are tightly closed. If you don't eat them right away, cover them with a damp towel but don't water them. You can also buy oysters already shucked. They should be plump, have a creamy color and be surrounded by clear liquid.

To shuck an oyster, protect your hand with heavy gloves, a potholder or a towel. Cutting your hand with the sharp edge of an oyster shell is not only painful, but can cause a bad infection. Place the oyster on a flat surface with the deep, rounded side down. Find the hinge, and insert the tip of an oyster knife between the top and bottom shells. Working carefully, pry the two shells slightly apart, then slide the oyster knife or a long slender blade between the oyster and the top shell and sever the muscle that connects them. Carefully remove the top shell so that you don't lose

any of the oyster liquor. Slide the knife under the oyster and cut the muscle connecting it to the bottom shell.

Oysters need very little cooking. For many recipes, the heat of a soup or gumbo that has been just removed from the stove is enough to cook the oyster. Cook only until the edges begin to curl. An overcooked oyster can take on the texture of leather.

SHRIMP. Use fresh shrimp whenever it is available. Frozen shrimp, which seems to be increasingly what is offered in seafood and grocery stores, can become mushy and flavorless. If you can find it, buy shrimp with the heads still on. The heads produce no meat but make wonderful stock. Asian markets frequently stock whole shrimp, or ask your grocer if whole shrimp can be special ordered. If a recipe calls for one pound of headless shrimp, buy two pounds of whole shrimp. The per-pound price of whole shrimp is typically about half the price of headless shrimp, so the total cost will be about the same. Most stores still sell shrimp in the shell, but the demands for convenience are prompting more stores to sell raw shrimp already shelled and deveined. Hold out for shrimp in the shell when you can. Even if you don't need stock for this recipe, you will probably want the shells to make stock in the next few weeks. Just freeze them until you need them.

To clean whole shrimp, cut off the tail right behind the head. Remove the legs and open the shell lengthwise, gently pulling it off at the end toward the head. You may leave the soft tail fins attached, if desired. To devein – especially in larger shrimp, where the vein tends to be gritty – make a shallow cut lengthwise down what looks like the back spine. Pull out the vein or wash it free.

FISH. Catfish, redfish, red snapper, speckled trout and pompano are the fish used most in Louisiana cooking, but in most Cajun-Creole recipes, you can substitute pretty freely similar fish that are available locally.

Catfish have become so popular that they are farmed in commercial ponds throughout the United States, although Mississippi is the biggest producer. There are about 20 species of catfish, but channel catfish, a white-fleshed, firm-textured, medium-oily fish, is the most common commercial species. Catfish have a tough, inedible skin that must be removed. Frying catfish is the most popular means of preparation, but it can also be served poached, steamed, baked, grilled or sauteed.

Pompano is a gourmet fish, delicious and very expensive. It lives in the Atlantic Ocean and the Caribbean. It is moderately fatty and firm textured, and does not fry well. It is excellent stuffed with crab and baked whole, or grilled. Substitute whole rainbow trout or flounder fillets.

Redfish is related to the Atlantic coast drum or croaker and the speckled trout of the Gulf. It became so popular in the 1980s as Cajun blackened redfish that it is now scarce in Gulf waters, and the state of Louisiana has temporarily banned its sale. It is a low-fat, firm-textured fish. As substitutes, try grouper (also known as sea bass), speckled trout, or other members of the drum/croaker family.

Red snapper is widely available along the Gulf and Atlantic coasts. It is a low-fat, firm-textured fish with vivid rose skin. Filleted, red snapper can be substituted for redfish and blackened. It is an adaptable fish that can be cooked a variety of ways. Substitutes include grouper (sea bass), tilefish, and redfish. Or, try orange roughy, a delicately flavored New Zealand fish.

Speckled trout has firm, white flesh and a delicate flavor and can be cooked many ways. Its size makes it perfect for single servings. Try it filleted and broiled. Other trout, including rainbow and brook trout, may be substituted, or try sea bass, orange roughy or flounder.

ANDOUILLE SAUSAGE is a spicy Cajun smoked-pork sausage. Some stores with gourmet delicatessen counters sell it, others offer what they call Cajun sausage or Louisiana sausage, which are not the same thing. You may substitute those or other sausages – Polish kielbasa is a good choice – but since Andouille supplies part of the spicy flavor in some recipes, be sure to adjust the seasonings if you use something else.

TASSO is very highly seasoned smoked pork or ham. It is rarely used as the star ingredient, but as a flavoring in jambalayas and other dishes. You may substitute another type of smoked ham, but add more cayenne and other seasonings if you want the dish to be spicy.

TABASCO SAUCE is the brand name of a Louisiana hot sauce made on Avery Island, deep in Cajun country. Very hot red peppers are ground with salt, fermented in oak barrels, then pickled with vinegar. Other manufacturers make similar hot-pepper sauces.

OPPOSITE A shrimp boat weighs anchor on the Louisiana bayou, which is home to many ingredients of Cajun cooking, including shrimp, alligator, wild turkeys, crawfish, and dozens of water birds and 85 species of fish.

THE BASICS

★

ROUX

Roux is a crucial ingredient in many Cajun dishes, including gumbo, crawfish étouffée, grillades and crawfish bisque. It is a thickener, but more important, it is a flavoring agent. A dark brown roux adds an incredible richness to a crawfish bisque, for example. Because of today's health concerns, I've reduced the quantity of roux used in some dishes, but left some in the recipes because of the flavor it adds.

≈ Roux is an ingredient to be treated with respect. It should be cooked slowly and must have constant attention. If the flour burns, you'll see black specks in the mixture. At that point, throw it out and start over. Otherwise, the scorched taste will permeate the food. If you don't use care, the roux may splatter you. If it does, its high temperature will raise blisters. That's why some call it "Cajun napalm."

≈ Roux is traditionally cooked over a low heat, with constant stirring or whisking. Made the traditional way, a dark mahogany roux will take 45 minutes to 1 hour to make. For the impatient, Paul Prudhomme recommends cooking quickly over high heat. But his method is too tricky for cooks unskilled in making roux. Start slowly, and adjust to your own pace. I use medium-low heat, and my dark roux requires about 25 minutes. Even so, the roux must be stirred constantly.

≈ Some people also recommend microwaving roux. I don't like this method as well because it has a greater tendency to become grainy. I have, however, included a recipe for microwave roux here.

≈ Even after you have removed roux from the heat, the high temperature in the fat will continue cooking the flour. The way to stop the cooking process is to stir in some or all of the chopped vegetables called for in the recipe.

≈ I prefer to use lard in my roux, but you may also use vegetable oil.

BASIC ROUX

BASIC ROUX:

1 cup lard
1 cup all-purpose flour

≈ In a heavy saucepan over medium-low to low heat, melt the lard. When it is hot, add about one-third of the flour at a time, whisking it until smooth each time. Continue stirring after all the flour is added. As the roux cooks, you will see the color darken and it will develop a nutty smell. Continue cooking until the roux reaches the desired color. DO NOT STOP STIRRING UNTIL THE ROUX IS DONE.

≈ When the roux reaches the desired color, remove it from the heat and stir in vegetables to stop the cooking. If no vegetables are called for, pour the roux into a metal bowl and continue stirring for 5-10 minutes until the darkening stops. At this point, you may return the roux and vegetables to the stock and continue the recipe, or set the roux aside and let it cool.

≈ Excess roux may be refrigerated or frozen.

PEANUT-BUTTER-COLORED ROUX   MEDIUM RED-BROWN ROUX   DARK, MAHOGANY-COLORED ROUX

MICROWAVE ROUX

≈ In an oven-tempered, 2-quart glass container, melt the lard. Whisk in the flour. Microwave on High power (100 percent) in 3-minute increments, stirring well after every increment. (The glass will be very hot.) Cook until the roux begins to separate and turn brown. Then microwave for 1-minute increments, stirring each time. When the roux reaches the desired color, stir in the chopped vegetables to stop the cooking, then continue with the recipe. Or, if you do not intend to add vegetables at this point, pour the roux into a bowl and continue stirring for 5-10 minutes.

STOCKS

Stock is the base upon which many Louisiana dishes are built. You can't make gumbos or most soups without it, and it is an important ingredient in various stews, pasta sauces and savory pie fillings. Sure, you can use canned broth or clam juice, but the richness of flavor of a long-simmered, homemade stock will be missing from the finished dish.

Making your own stock means you cannot take advantage of some of the convenience of today's meat and seafood products. It's difficult to find shrimp with the heads on, for example, and more stores are catering to working men and women by offering shrimp already shelled and deveined. Yes, it is a lot of work to crack and clean your own crabs, and the task seems especially daunting if you do not need seafood stock to go with that crab. But that carcass will be invaluable next week or the week after. When you buy cut-up chicken, make sure the package includes the back and neck. Then freeze those shrimp and crab shells, the carcass of last night's roast duck, the neck and back from the chicken, the bones from the rib roast. Save them until you have an afternoon when you can let them simmer for hours on the back burner.

If you know you'll be making stock in a few days, don't throw away the limp carrot, the celery leaves or the nearly naked parsley stems. Save them in a plastic bag for stock, where the aesthetics of your vegetables are not important, just their flavor. And parsley stems and celery leaves have lots of flavor.

Some tips:

≈ Bell peppers, bloody fish parts and livers give stock a bad taste. Do not use them.

≈ Do not salt your stock. As the stock reduces, the salty flavor will intensify.

≈ Do not add chopped herbs or spices until you're ready to cook with the stock, or you may skim them off when you remove fat or foam. (Obviously, that is not a problem with whole items such as bay leaves, sprigs of fresh herbs, cloves and peppercorns.)

≈ For safety reasons, do not refrigerate stock longer than two days. For reasons of taste, do not freeze it longer than six months.

POULTRY AND GAME STOCK

Use 2 pounds, any combination, of backs, necks and bones from chickens, ducks, rabbits, geese, etc. Do not use livers If you have time, roast the bones at 350° for about 40 minutes. This will give the stock a richer flavor. You may also add trimmings from any other vegetable – except bell peppers – you are using in a particular recipe.

MAKES 1 QUART

| 1 onion, cut into chunks |
| 1 celery stalk, leaves included, sliced |
| 1 garlic clove, crushed |
| 1 carrot, unpeeled, cut into chunks. |
| 1 sprig fresh parsley |
| 5 whole black peppercorns |

≈ Put all ingredients in a large pot. Add 1 quart water. Make a mental note of the water level in the pot, because you want to have at least 1 quart of stock after it has simmered for several hours. Add another 1 quart of water, enough to cover the bones and vegetables by several inches. Bring to a full boil. Skim off any gray foam. Reduce the heat and simmer for at least 4 hours, adding extra water if necessary to keep at least 1 quart liquid in the pot.

≈ Strain the stock, discarding the bones and vegetables. If you plan to use immediately, skim the fat from the top. Otherwise, cool and refrigerate. Stock should be cooled quickly to avoid spoiling, but should not be put directly from the stove into the refrigerator. Run 2–3 inches of cold water into the sink, and add ice if you want. Pour the stock into small containers. As soon as the stock comes close to room temperature, refrigerate. After several hours, the fat will have congealed on top and can be removed easily. Freeze or return to the refrigerator.

BROWN MEAT STOCK

Use 2 pounds, any combination, of necks and bones from beef, veal and/or pork. If you have time, roast the bones at 350° until thoroughly browned. This will give stock a richer flavor. You may also add trimmings from any other vegetable – except bell peppers – you are using in a particular recipe.

MAKES 1 QUART

| 1 onion, cut into chunks |
| 1 celery stalk, leaves included, sliced |
| 1 garlic clove, unpeeled, cut into chunks |
| 1 sprig fresh parsley |
| 5 whole black peppercorns |

≈ Put all ingredients in a large pot. Add 1 quart water. Make a mental note of the water level in the pot, because you want to have at least 1 quart of stock after it has simmered for several hours. Add another 1 quart of water, enough to cover the bones and vegetables by several inches. Bring mixture to a boil. Skim off any gray foam. Reduce the heat and simmer for at least 4 hours, adding water if necessary, to keep at least 1 quart liquid in the pot.

≈ Strain the stock, discarding the bones and vegetables. If you plan to use immediately, skin the fat from the top. Otherwise, cool and refrigerate. Stock should be cooled quickly to avoid spoiling, but shouldn't be put directly from the stove into the refrigerator. Run 2–3 inches of cold water into the sink, and add ice if you want. Pour the stock into small containers and place the containers in the sink. As soon as the stock comes close to room temperature, refrigerate. After it has been in the refrigerator for several hours, the fat will have congealed on the top and can be removed easily. Freeze or return to refrigerator.

SEAFOOD STOCK

Use 2 pounds, any combination, of shrimp shells and heads, crab shells, crawfish heads and shells, lobster carcasses and fish carcasses with heads and gills removed. You may also add oyster liquor. You may also add trimmings from any other vegetable – except bell peppers – you are using in a particular recipe.

MAKES 1 QUART

1 onion, cut into chunks
1 celery stalk, leaves included, sliced
1 garlic clove, crushed
1 carrot, unpeeled, cut into chunks
1 sprig fresh parsley
5 whole black peppercorns

≈ Put all ingredients in a large pot. Add 1 quart water. Make a mental note of the water level in the pot, because you want to have at least 1 quart of stock after it has simmered for several hours. Add another 1 quart of water, enough to cover the shells and vegetables by several inches. Bring to a full boil. Skim off the gray foam. Reduce the heat and simmer for at least 4 hours, adding extra water if necessary, to keep at least 1 quart liquid in the pot.

≈ Strain the stock, discarding the shells and vegetables. If you are not using immediately, cool and refrigerate. Stock should be cooled quickly to avoid spoiling, but should not be put directly from the stove into the refrigerator. Run 2–3 inches of cold water into the sink, and add ice if you want. Pour the stock into small containers and place the containers in the sink. As soon as the stock comes close to room temperature, refrigerate or freeze.

APPETIZERS

---★---

OYSTERS ROCKEFELLER

An elegant dish for oyster lovers that combines the mellow tastes of oysters and spinach. Louisiana cooks used to flavor this with absinthe, a licorice-flavored liqueur that's been outlawed in the United States. I've used aniseed, but you could also substitute Pernod or any other aniseed-flavored liqueur.

SERVES 4

rock salt
¼ cup butter
2½ cups chopped fresh spinach
¼ cup chopped fresh parsley
6 green onions, chopped
2 tbsp. finely chopped celery
1 tbsp. finely chopped green pepper
¼ tsp. salt
¼ tsp. aniseed
1½ tsp. fresh thyme or ½ tsp. dried
1 tbsp. anchovy paste
¼ cup dry bread crumbs
½ cup heavy cream
pinch of fresh ground black pepper
few drops of Tabasco sauce
20 oysters on the half shells

OVEN TEMPERATURE: 400°

≈ Pour the rock salt about ½ inch deep into a large baking pan, and put into the oven at 400°. The salt serves to keep the oysters from tipping over, and it will help keep them warm after they come out of the oven.

≈ In a skillet over low heat, melt the butter. Saute the spinach, parsley, onions, celery and green pepper until the spinach is thoroughly wilted, about 6 minutes. Add remaining ingredients, except the oysters, stirring in a little extra cream or bread crumbs as needed to achieve the consistency of a thick sauce.

≈ Put 1 oyster on each half shelf and spoon some of the sauce over each oyster. Nestle the oysters in the heated rock salt. Bake at 400° until the topping is bubbly, about 12 minutes.

OYSTERS BIENVILLE

Shrimps, mushrooms and Parmesan cheese create a delicious topping that is a truly wonderful complement to the delicate oyster taste. This dish is named for Jean Baptiste le Moyne, Sieur de Bienville, the founder of New Orleans.

SERVES 3–4

rock salt
2 tbsp. butter
3 green onions, minced
2 cloves garlic, minced
1 tbsp. minced fresh parsley
4 large mushrooms, finely chopped
2 tbsp. all-purpose flour
¾ cup heavy cream
¼ lb. shrimp, shelled, deveined, cooked and minced
1 egg yolk, lightly beaten
1 tbsp. dry sherry
⅛ tsp. black pepper
⅛ tsp. cayenne
1 tsp. Worcestershire sauce
pinch of salt
6 tbsp. grated Parmesan cheese
2 tbsp. dry bread crumbs
¼ tsp. salt
⅛ tsp. cayenne
⅛ tsp. black pepper
16 oysters on the half shell

OVEN TEMPERATURE: 400°

≈ Pour the rock salt about ½ inch deep into a large baking pan, or several pans, large enough to hold all the oysters in a single layer, and put it into the oven at 400°. The salt serves to keep the oysters from tipping over, and will help keep them warm after they come out of the oven.

≈ In a skillet over a moderate heat, melt the butter. Saute the green onions, garlic, parsley and mushrooms until the vegetables are limp, about 5 minutes. Add the flour and stir until blended. Add the cream and stir until blended. Add the shrimp, egg yolk, sherry, black pepper, cayenne, Worcestershire and salt and cook until the mixture thickens, stirring, 5–6 minutes.

≈ In a small bowl, make the crumb topping mixture. Combine the Parmesan, bread crumbs, salt, cayenne and pepper.

≈ Put 1 oyster on each half shell and spoon some shrimp sauce over each oyster. Top each with the crumb mixture. Nestle the oysters in hot rock salt. Bake at 400° until the topping is golden, 12–15 minutes.

ELEGANT DINNER

★

Oysters Rockefeller
PAGE 19

★

Oysters Bienville
PAGES 20–21

★

Cream of Artichoke Soup
PAGE 43

★

Crab-Stuffed Fish
PAGE 62

★

Steamed broccoli and carrots

★

Trinity Rice with Almonds
PAGES 98–99

★

Peach Tart with Raspberry Filling
PAGE 110

DEEP-FRIED OYSTERS

Even people who don't eat oysters will love these hot, crisp finger foods. Cooked quickly at high heat, the delicate and juicy flavor of the oysters is sealed in. Corn flour can be found in many natural food stores. You may use cornmeal in place of the corn flour, and the result will be a slightly coarser, heavier, but still delicious, coating.

SERVES 4–6

1 cup cornmeal
½ cup corn flour
1 tsp. salt
½ tsp. black pepper
½ tsp. cayenne
2 dozen fresh oysters, shucked
vegetable oil for frying

≈ Combine all the ingredients, except the oysters and oil. Pat the oysters dry with paper towels, then dip the oysters in the cornmeal mixture.

≈ In a deep skillet or wok, heat the oil to 365°. With tongs, drop in 4 or 5 oysters at a time and cook until golden brown, turning once and making sure they don't touch, about 3 minutes. Drain well on paper towels and keep warm while you fry the remaining oysters. Make sure the oil has returned to 365° before cooking each batch. Serve hot with Cocktail Sauce (page 121) for dipping the oysters into.

MUSHROOMS WITH SHRIMP-CORNBREAD STUFFING

These mushrooms, served hot, make a tasty snack or a first course. You may substitute crawfish tails for the shrimp. If you're making Crawfish Bisque (pages 43–45), make some extra stuffing and add spices (the stuffing in the bisque picks up its flavor from the broth), then use it in these mushrooms.

MAKES 24

24 medium to large mushrooms
2 tbsp. butter
½ cup chopped onion
¼ cup chopped green onion
¼ cup chopped green pepper
1 rib celery, chopped
2 cloves garlic, minced
2 tbsp. chopped fresh parsley
1 tsp. fresh thyme or ¼ tsp. dried
½ tsp. salt
¼ tsp. black pepper
¼ tsp. cayenne
½ tsp. dry mustard
1 tsp. lemon juice
1 egg, lightly beaten
2 cups finely crumbled cornbread (pages 96–97)
4 oz. small cooked shrimp, shelled and coarsely chopped
seafood stock (page 17) or milk to moisten

OVEN TEMPERATURE: 350°

≈ Clean the mushrooms and separate the stems from the caps. Discard the stems or save for another use. Steam the mushroom caps for 5 minutes, then set aside.

≈ In medium skillet, melt the butter over low heat. Saute the onions, pepper, celery and garlic until limp, about 5 minutes. Put in a medium bowl. Add the remaining ingredients, except the stock or milk, then mix well. Add enough stock or milk so the mixture is thoroughly moistened, but not mushy.

≈ Stuff the mushroom caps with the shrimp mixture, mounding a little on each top. Arrange on lightly greased baking sheet. Bake at 350° until stuffing is lightly browned, 10–15 minutes. Serve hot.

LEFT *The French Quarter was the birthplace of New Orleans and still retains the narrow streets that were laid out by the French. Its carefully restored buildings, many of them* more than a century old, are noted for their balconies and intimate courtyards. The French Quarter is alive with jazz clubs, antique shops and world-famous restaurants.

PAN-FRIED OYSTERS

These pan-fried oysters are almost as delicious as deep-fried oysters, but not quite as intimidating for someone who is not adept at deep-frying.

SERVES 3–4

½ cup all-purpose flour
¾ cup dry bread crumbs
½ tsp. salt
½ tsp. black pepper
½ tsp. cayenne
¼ tsp. dried thyme
2 eggs, lightly beaten
2 tbsp. milk
2 dozen fresh oysters, shucked
butter for frying

≈ Combine the flour, bread crumbs, salt, pepper, cayenne and thyme. In another bowl, combine the eggs and milk.

≈ Pat the oysters dry with paper towels. Quickly dip the oysters in the crumb mixture, then in the egg mixture, then again in the crumbs.

≈ In a skillet, melt 2–3 tablespoons butter. Fry some oysters in a single layer until lightly browned on one side, then turn over and cook until other side is lightly browned. Remove from the skillet and keep warm while you fry the remaining oysters. Add a little more butter to the skillet and fry next batch. Continue until all the oysters are fried. Serve the oysters with lemon wedges and Cocktail Sauce (page 121).

TWO-BITE MEAT PIES

You can fill these savory miniature turnovers with almost anything – Dirty Rice (page 78), Crawfish Pie filling (page 55), or the fillings listed below. Once filled these can be baked or fried, but I recommend the lower-fat baked version. Serve these hot for snacking during card games or football-watching parties.

MAKES ABOUT 24 PIES

PASTRY

2½ cups all-purpose flour
pinch of salt
4 tbsp. cold butter
4 tbsp. lard
2 eggs, lightly beaten
3–4 tbsp. cold milk

GLAZE

1 egg, lightly beaten
¼ cup milk

OVEN TEMPERATURE: 375°

≈ Sift together the flour and salt. Using a pastry cutter or a pair of sharp knives, cut in the shortenings until the flour is the consistency of cornmeal. Add the eggs and mix well. Add the milk, 1 tablespoon at a time, until the dough sticks together and forms a ball.

≈ Wrap the dough in plastic wrap and refrigerate for at least 1 hour. Meanwhile, make the filling of your choice.

≈ Return dough to room temperature before rolling out.

≈ Roll out the dough ⅛ inch thick. With cutter or inverted glass, cut the dough into circles 3–4 inches in diameter. Gather up the scraps, roll out again and cut out circles, repeating until all the dough is all used.

≈ Put 1 tablespoon filling in the center of each circle. Fold each circle in half, pinch the edges together to seal.

≈ Place each on lightly greased baking sheet. Mix the egg and milk together, and brush across tops of the pies. Bake at 375° until the pastry is lightly browned, about 20 minutes. Serve hot.

IF YOU USE A FOOD PROCESSOR:

≈ Mix all the ingredients together, except the milk. Then place the dough into a bowl, add 1 tablespoon of milk at a time and mix gently with your hands until dough sticks together and forms a ball. If you add the milk in the food processor, you won't be able to feel when the dough is moist enough, and will probably add too much milk.

SPICY PORK AND BEEF FILLING

For a spicier filling, substitute a jalapeño chili for the mild one specified in the recipe.

ENOUGH FILLING FOR ABOUT 24 PIES

2 tbsp. vegetable oil
1 onion, chopped
3 cloves garlic, minced
1 mild chili, chopped
½ lb. ground pork
½ lb. ground beef
1 tomato, seeded and chopped
1 cup grated raw potato
1 tsp. salt
1 tsp. ground cumin
1½ tsp. fresh thyme or ½ tsp. dried
1½ tsp. fresh oregano or ½ tsp. dried
2 tbsp. chopped fresh cilantro
¾ cup beef stock (page 16)

≈ In large skillet, heat the oil. Saute the onion, garlic and chili until onion is golden, about 10 minutes. Add the meat and cook until browned. Add the tomato, potato, seasonings and stock and mix well. Lower the heat and simmer 10 minutes. Taste and adjust the seasonings. Set aside and let cool before using.

PORK AND TASSO FILLING

This is a chunky filling in a spicy, savory sauce.

ENOUGH FILLING FOR ABOUT 24 PIES

2 tbsp. vegetable oil
1 lb pork, diced into ¼-inch pieces
4 oz. Tasso, diced
½ cup lard
½ cup all-purpose flour
1 cup chopped onion
½ cup chopped celery
½ cup chopped green pepper
2½ cups beef stock
¼ tsp. dried sage
¼ tsp. cayenne
¼ tsp. black pepper
2 tsp. fresh thyme or ½ tsp. dried
2 tsp. dry mustard

≈ In a medium skillet, heat the oil. Saute the pork and Tasso until browned. Set aside.

≈ In medium saucepan, make a peanut-butter-colored roux of the lard and flour (page 15). Remove from the heat and stir in the vegetables. Return to the heat and cook until the vegetables are wilted, about 5 minutes.

≈ In a small saucepan, bring the beef stock to a boil and add the seasonings. Gradually add the stock to the roux, whisking after each addition. Stir in the pork and Tasso. Simmer until mixture is slightly thickened, about 15 minutes. Set aside and let cool before using.

CRAB-STUFFED MUSHROOMS

These mushrooms are very rich and very delicious. Even people who usually think they do not like seafood will love this stuffing.

MAKES 24

24 large fresh mushrooms
2 tbsp. butter
4 green onions, chopped
1 clove garlic, minced
1/2 tsp. salt
1/2 tsp. cayenne
1/4 cup dry bread crumbs
1/4 cup heavy cream or half-and-half
3/4 lb. fresh crab meat, picked over, or frozen or canned, well drained
Parmesan cheese

OVEN TEMPERATURE: 350°

≈ Clean the mushrooms and separate the stems from the caps. Meanwhile, finely chop the stems. Steam the mushrooms for 5 minutes, then set aside.

≈ In a skillet over medium heat, melt the butter. Add the chopped stems, green onions and garlic and cook until most of the liquid is evaporated, 8–10 minutes. Add the salt, cayenne, bread crumbs and cream, and mix well. Gently stir in the crab meat and cook until just heated through.

≈ Stuff the mushroom caps with the crab mixture, mounding a little on each top. Sprinkle each with Parmesan cheese. Arrange on a lightly greased baking sheet. Bake at 350° for 10 minutes, then broil 2–3 minutes until the cheese turns golden brown.

FROGS' LEGS

These frogs' legs are dipped in two breading mixtures, then quickly deep-fried in very hot oil so they don't become greasy. I like to serve them as appetizers, with tartar sauce on the side, but I serve more than one appetizer so my more squeamish friends – the ones who aren't reassured that frogs' legs taste like chicken – have something to eat.

SERVES 6–12 AS APPETIZERS

2 lbs. frogs' legs
2 cups all-purpose flour
1 tsp. salt
½ tsp. black pepper
½ tsp. cayenne
1 tsp. onion powder
1 tsp. garlic powder
2 eggs, lightly beaten
¾ cup milk
1½ cups cornmeal
¾ cup corn flour
1 tsp. salt
¼ tsp. black pepper
¼ tsp. cayenne
vegetable oil for frying

≈ Wash the frogs' legs and pat dry on paper towels. Set aside.

≈ Set out 3 bowls. In the first bowl, combine the all-purpose flour, salt, pepper, cayenne and onion and garlic powders. In the second bowl, mix the eggs and milk, together. In the third bowl, combine the cornmeal and remaining ingredients, except the oil.

≈ Dip the frogs' legs first in flour mixture, then shake off the excess. Next, dip the frogs' legs in the egg mixture, then in the cornmeal mixture, again shaking off the excess.

≈ In a deep skillet or wok, heat 2–3 inches of oil to 360°. Fry the frogs' legs in small batches so they are not crowded. Cook for 7 minutes, turning once. Remove from the oil, drain briefly, then place on paper towels and keep warm in the oven while you fry the remaining frogs' legs. Make sure the oil returns to 360° before frying the next batch.

RIGHT Located in northeastern Louisiana near St. Joseph, Lake Bruin was developed as a State Park in the 1950s around a beautiful oxbow lake, once part of the Mississippi River. The park is famed for the old cypress trees growing from the lake itself and for its excellent fishing and boating waters.

CAJUN POPCORN

Little shrimp or crawfish tails are dipped in a spicy flour batter, then deep fried to make these tasty tidbits. Serve with Tartar Sauce (page 121), Mustard Sauce (pages 122–123) or Cocktail Sauce (page 121) for dipping. And, be sure to make plenty.

SERVES 6–8

¾ cup corn flour
¾ cup all-purpose flour
2 tbsp. cornmeal
1 tsp. salt
½ tsp. onion powder
½ tsp. garlic powder
¼ tsp. cayenne
⅛ tsp. black pepper
2 eggs, lightly beaten
1 tbsp. butter, melted
¾ cup warm beer
2 lbs. small shrimp, shelled and deveined, or crawfish tails, shelled
vegetable oil for frying

≈ Combine all the dry ingredients. Whisk in the eggs, butter and beer until smooth. Refrigerate at least 3 hours to give the gluten in the flour a chance to expand. Whisk again before serving.

≈ In a deep skillet or wok heat 1½ inches of oil to 350°. Pat the shrimp dry, then dip in the batter. Drop some of the shrimp in the oil, but don't crowd, and fry until golden brown, turning once, about 2 minutes total. Drain well on paper towels and keep warm while frying the remaining shrimp. Be sure the oil returns to 350° before frying the next batch. Continue until all the shrimp are fried.

SHRIMP SALSA

SHRIMP SALSA

A cool, easy dip for crackers, chips or vegetables. Make a couple hours in advance to let the flavors blend. Taste again just before serving and adjust the Tabasco sauce. For a hot salsa, use a jalapeño chili.

2 medium tomatoes, seeded and chopped
1/2 cucumber, peeled, seeded and diced
3 green onions, finely chopped
1 mild chili, seeded and finely chopped
2 tbsp. chopped fresh cilantro
1½ tbsp. olive oil
1½ tbsp. cider vinegar
dash of salt
few drops of Tabasco sauce
¼ lb. tiny shrimp, cooked and cleaned

≈ In a bowl, combine all the ingredients and refrigerate for at least 2 hours before serving.

HOT CRAB SPREAD

This creamy dip, served hot, is delicious with crackers or raw vegetables. And, it's easy to make. I recommend fresh crab meat but frozen or canned are acceptable.

3 tbsp. sour cream
3 oz. cream cheese
1 tbsp. fresh-squeezed lemon juice
½ tsp. prepared horseradish
1 tbsp. chopped fresh dill
2 green onions, finely minced
dash of salt
dash of fresh-ground black pepper
6 oz. fresh crab meat, picked over

OVEN TEMPERATURE: 350°

≈ Cream the sour cream and cream cheese together with an electric beater. Add the remaining ingredients, except the crab, and beat until smooth. Gently stir in the crab.
≈ Put the mixture in an ovenproof serving dish and bake at 350° until hot, about 15 minutes. Serve immediately.

CAJUN DEVILED EGGS

HOT CRAB SPREAD

CAJUN DEVILED EGGS

The Tasso gives these deviled eggs their spicy taste. If you don't have Tasso, use another ham, but add cayenne and paprika to give it a Cajun flavor.

MAKES 6

6 eggs, hard-boiled and shelled
1 oz. Tasso, minced
1 tbsp. minced green pepper
1 green onion, finely chopped
½ tsp. fresh-squeezed lemon juice
2 tbsp. mayonnaise
2 tbsp. Dijon-style mustard
dash of fresh-ground pepper
1–2 drops of Tabasco sauce

≈ Cut the eggs in half lengthwise. Remove the yolks and put them in a small bowl and set aside the whites. Mash the yolks with a fork. Add the remaining ingredients to the yolks and mix well with a fork. Taste and adjust the seasonings. Spoon the mixture into the egg whites.

COLD SHRIMP IN HORSERADISH SAUCE

These pungent, spicy shrimp are easy to make and have the advantage of being prepared in advance. Serve as an appetizer, with lots of toothpicks and napkins on the side.

SERVES 4–6

2 tbsp. cider vinegar
2 tbsp. lemon juice
¼ cup olive oil
2 cloves garlic, minced
¼ cup chopped green onions
2 tbsp. minced fresh parsley
1 tsp. red-pepper flakes
1 tsp. Creole mustard
2 tbsp. Dijon-style mustard
2 tbsp. prepared horseradish
½ tsp. celery seed
1 lb. medium cooked shrimp, shelled and deveined

≈ In a bowl, combine all the ingredients, except the shrimp, and mix well. Add the shrimp, making sure each piece is well coated. Refrigerate for at least 3 hours or as long as 24 hours.

CAJUN BBQ SHRIMP

It is a tradition of Cajun cooking that BBQ shrimp never see a grill. Instead, they are briefly cooked in a buttery sauce so spicy that the shells are left on during cooking, as protection for the diner, and then peeled by hand as they are eaten. I like to serve these as an appetizer, with lots of bread on the side for dipping in the leftover sauce. Although this recipe is spicy hot, it is not as palate-searing as some Cajun recipes.

SERVES 6–8

1½ cups unsalted butter
6 garlic cloves, minced
1 tbsp. chopped fresh basil or 1 tsp. dried
2 tsp. fresh rosemary or ½ tsp. dried
1½ tsp. fresh oregano or ½ tsp. dried
1 cup seafood stock (page 17)
4 tsp. fresh-squeezed lemon juice
1 tbsp. Worcestershire sauce
½ tsp. salt
2 tsp. cayenne
1 tsp. paprika
2 tsp. dry mustard
1 tsp. red-pepper flakes
1½ lbs. medium unshelled shrimp

≈ In a heavy saucepan over low heat, melt the butter, swirling occasionally and taking care that butter does not brown. As soon as the butter starts to melt, add the garlic and herbs, and continue swirling until butter is completely melted.

≈ Add the remaining ingredients, except the shrimp, and use a wire whisk to mix well. Simmer over low heat to allow flavors to blend, about 15 minutes. Add the shrimp and cook just until shrimp are opaque and curled, 5–7 minutes. Remove from heat and pour carefully into a heat-proof serving dish.

SALADS

— ★ —

TOMATO-BASIL SALAD

Take advantage of the ripe tomatoes and surplus of basil from summer gardens with this cool and elegant – but simple – salad. Drizzle with Vinagrette (page 123), a combination of balsamic vinegar and a high-quality olive oil, or your favorite dressing.

SERVES 4

4 large, ripe tomatoes, sliced
bunch of fresh basil
4–6 thin slices of red onion, or 1 of the sweet onions such as Vidalia or Walla Walla
salt to taste
fresh-ground black papper

≈ Slice the tomatoes, salt lightly, and let them drain on paper towels for about 20 minutes.

≈ Wash the basil and dry well with paper towels or in a salad spinner. Tear the leaves from the stems and arrange a thin layer of leaves on a platter. Top with about half the tomato slices. Separate the onion rings and scatter about half over the tomatoes. Add another layer of basil, tomatoes and onions. Sprinkle lightly with fresh-ground black pepper, and garnish with a few extra basil leaves.

VARIATION:

≈ Top the tomatoes with thin slices of fresh mozzarella cheese.

SHRIMP SALAD

This chilled salad uses shrimp, artichoke hearts and olives, and is topped with a creamy and tangy, but reduced-calorie, dressing.

SERVES 4

Lettuce, spinach, or a combination of both
1 lb. shrimp, cooked, shelled, deveined and chilled
2 large or 3 medium whole artichoke hearts, cooked, chilled and sliced
3 oz. pitted ripe olives
2 ripe tomatoes, cut into wedges
1 cup sliced mushrooms

DRESSING

¾ cup low-fat plain yogurt
3 tbsp. mayonnaise, preferably reduced-calorie
3 tbsp. buttermilk
1½ tsp. fresh-squeezed lemon juice
1 green onion, minced
2 tbsp. Dijon-style mustard
salt to taste
fresh-ground white pepper to taste

≈ To make the dressing, whisk all the ingredients together and refrigerate until ready to serve. The dressing tastes better if you allow several hours for flavors to blend.

≈ Arrange a bed of greens on each of 4 salad plates. Divide the shrimp, artichoke slices, olives, tomatoes, and mushrooms among the 4 plates and top with the dressing and fresh-ground black pepper, if desired.

BELOW *The Blessing of the Fleet at the annual festival held in Morgan City to honor the* economic lifeblood of the area — the shrimp and petroleum industries.

CORN SALAD

Marinated and served cold, this salad is a great way to use up any leftover vegetable in your refrigerator. Use fresh corn if it's available, or substitute frozen corn.

SERVES 6

3 cups corn kernels (7–8 fresh ears)
½ cup thinly sliced carrot
1½ cup thinly sliced zucchini
12 cherry tomatoes, halved
1 green pepper, chopped
½ small red onion, thinly sliced
3-oz. can ripe olives, drained
1 tbsp. capers

DRESSING

6 tbsp. olive oil
3 tbsp. white wine vinegar
1 tsp. fresh lemon juice
1 tsp. Dijon-style mustard
1 tbsp. fresh tarragon
½ tsp. salt
¼ tsp. black pepper
⅛ tsp. cayenne

≈ Cook corn in boiling water until tender, about 3 minutes, then drain. Rinse with cold water and drain again. Mix with all the salad ingredients in a bowl.

≈ In a bottle or small bowl, mix together all the dressing ingredients. Shake or whisk to mix thoroughly. Pour over salad and stir to coat. Refrigerate several hours.

COLESLAW

This tangy cabbage salad provides a cool counterpart to Fried Catfish (page 59), Cajun BBQ Shrimp (pages 30–31) or Blackened Redfish (pages 56–57). Use a combination of red and white cabbage for color. Prepare this several hours in advance to give flavors time to blend.

SERVES 4

4 cups shredded cabbage
3 carrots, peeled and grated
3 green onions, minced
½ large green pepper, cut into thin strips
½ cup mayonnaise
½ cup sour cream
¼ cup white wine vinegar
1 tbsp. sugar
1 tbsp. chopped fresh parsley
1 tsp. celery seed
1 tbsp. grated onion
pinch of salt
pinch of fresh-ground black pepper

≈ In a salad bowl, combine the vegetables and toss together well.

≈ In a small bowl, whisk together the remaining ingredients, then taste and adjust seasonings. Mix with the slaw, cover and refrigerate until ready to serve.

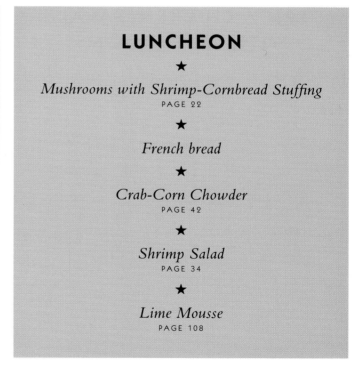

LUNCHEON

★

Mushrooms with Shrimp-Cornbread Stuffing
PAGE 22

★

French bread

★

Crab-Corn Chowder
PAGE 42

★

Shrimp Salad
PAGE 34

★

Lime Mousse
PAGE 108

SPICY CHICKEN SALAD WITH MUSHROOMS

SPICY CHICKEN SALAD WITH MUSHROOMS

The subtle taste of mushrooms, the tang of oranges and the nutty taste of pecans complement the spicy chicken in this salad.

SERVES 4

1 tsp. salt
1/2 tsp. cayenne
1/2 tsp. black pepper
3/4 tsp. fresh thyme
1 uncooked chicken breast, skinned and cut into strips
2 tbsp. vegetable oil
4 cups torn lettuce or salad greens
1 cup sliced mushrooms
1/2 cup pecans
2 Satsuma oranges, sectioned, or one 11-oz. can mandarin orange

≈ In a small bowl, mix the spices together. Toss the chicken in the spices, until chicken is well coated.

≈ In a skillet, heat the oil, saute the chicken until brown all over. Drain well on paper towels and refrigerate the chicken until ready to serve.

≈ In a salad bowl, toss the greens, mushrooms, pecans, oranges and chicken. Serve with a favorite dressing.

POTATO SALAD

Sour cream and fresh dill flavor this salad made with unpeeled potatoes. You can serve it chilled, but I like it best when the potatoes are still slightly warm so the flavors are not masked.

SERVES 6–8

2 lbs. small red potatoes, unpeeled
1/2 cup mayonnaise
1 cup sour cream
1/2 tsp. salt
1/4 tsp. black pepper
1/2 tsp. dry mustard
2 tbsp. chopped fresh parsley
2 tbsp. chopped fresh dill
1 stalk celery, diced
4 green onions, chopped
3 hard-boiled eggs, diced

≈ Drop the potatoes into boiling water and cook until fork tender, 20–30 minutes, depending on their size. Drain well and let sit until cool enough to handle.

≈ While the potatoes are cooking, make a dressing by whisking together the mayonnaise, sour cream, salt, pepper, mustard, parsley and dill. Set aside to let the flavors blend.

≈ Cube the potatoes and mix with the celery, onions and eggs. Gently stir in the dressing. Taste and adjust seasonings.

COLD JAMBALAYA SALAD

This salad is a great make-ahead dish, and a great way to use up leftovers. For an elegant presentation, mound the salad on a serving platter or a pretty ceramic tart pan, then circle it with wedges of tomatoes and/or lemons, and top it with several large cooked shrimp and a sprig of parsley.

SERVES 6

1 tbsp. butter
½ cup chopped onions
1 clove garlic, minced
¼ cup diced cooked ham
1 tsp. salt
¼ tsp. cayenne
1 bay leaf
1 cup white rice
2 tbsp. good-quality olive oil
1 tbsp. wine or balsamic vinegar
1 tbsp. fresh-squeezed lemon juice
few drops of Tabasco sauce, if desired
3 green onions, chopped
2 ribs celery, chopped
½ cup chopped green pepper
2 medium tomatoes, seeded and cut into bite-size chunks
1½ lbs. any combination of cooked shrimp, crab or chicken

≈ In a medium saucepan, melt the butter. Saute the onions and garlic until wilted, about 5 minutes. Add 2 cups water, the ham and seasonings, and bring to a boil. Stir in the rice and return to a boil. Reduce the heat to very low, cover and cook until liquid is absorbed and the top of the rice is pitted with steam holes, 15–20 minutes. Fluff the rice with a fork. Cover, remove from the heat and let sit for 5–10 minutes. Chill or let sit until cold. Remove the bay leaf.

≈ In a large bowl, toss the rice with the olive oil, vinegar, and lemon juice. Taste and adjust flavorings, and add Tabasco sauce if desired. Stir in the remaining ingredients, garnish and serve.

SOUPS AND STEWS

—★—

OYSTER STEW

Essentially oysters cooked in cream, this rich 'stew' is deceptively easy.

SERVES 4

2 tbsp. butter
4 green onions, finely chopped
¼ cup finely chopped celery
1 qt. half-and-half
½ tsp. salt
¼ tsp. cayenne
2 tsp. Worcestershire sauce
3 dozen large or 4 dozen small-medium oysters with their liquor, large oysters halved
butter or sherry for garnishing

≈ In a medium saucepan over low heat, melt the butter. Saute the green onions and celery until limp, about 5 minutes.

≈ Add the half-and-half, salt, cayenne and Worcestershire sauce and heat until the soup just starts to boil. Lower the heat, add the oysters and their liquor, and cook just until the edges of the oysters start to curl, 2–3 minutes. Taste and adjust the seasonings.

≈ You may garnish each bowl with a pat of butter or a dash of sherry, if you like.

SHRIMP AND LEEK BISQUE

This rich, creamy bisque starts with a flavorful shrimp stock, so buy shrimp with the heads on if you can find them. It's important to make your own stock for this soup, so it picks up the delicate flavor of leeks. If you can't find shrimp with heads, get some extra shells to make the stock with. I like to make the soup, up through the point of pureeing, early in the day, then reheat and add the cream just before serving.

SERVES 6

¾ lb. medium shrimp, shelled and deveined with heads and shells reserved
1 large carrot, unpeeled, cut into chunks
2 celery ribs, leaves and all, sliced
2 leeks, including green tops, sliced
2–3 sprigs of fresh parsley
2 bay leaves
5 black peppercorns
3 tbsp. butter
1 leek, white part only, chopped
2 cloves garlic, minced
3 cups sliced mushrooms
2 tbsp. minced fresh parsley
1 bay leaf
1 tsp. salt
2 tsp. chopped fresh basil
1 tsp. chopped fresh thyme
⅛ tsp. white pepper
⅛ tsp. black pepper
⅛ tsp. cayenne
½ tsp. dry mustard
3 tbsp. all-purpose flour
1½ cups heavy cream
2 tbsp. sherry

≈ Put the shrimp heads and shells, carrot, celery, leeks, parsley, bay leaves and peppercorns in a large pot. Add 1 quart water. Make a mental note of the water level in the pot, because you will want to have at least 1 quart of stock after it has simmered for several hours. Add another 1–2 quarts water, enough to cover the shrimp shells and vegetables by several inches. Bring to a full boil. Skim off the gray foam. Reduce the heat and simmer, uncovered, for 2–3 hours, adding extra water if necessary to keep at least 1 quart of liquid in the pot.

≈ Strain the stock, discarding the shrimp heads, shells and vegetables. Measure 1 quart stock into a small saucepan; freeze or refrigerate any remaining stock for future use. Return 1 quart of stock to the stove and keep warm over low heat.

≈ In a skillet, melt the butter. Saute the leek, garlic and mushrooms about 10 minutes. Add the vegetables to the stock with the seasonings. Bring to a boil, then reduce the heat and simmer, uncovered, 15 minutes. Add the shrimp and simmer just until shrimp are opaque and tightly curled.

≈ Puree the soup in a blender or food processor; you will probably have to do this in several batches. (At this point you may refrigerate the pureed soup for several hours. Reheat before continuing.)

≈ Whisk the flour into the cream, then add to the soup. Heat just short of the boiling point. Taste and adjust seasonings. Add the sherry.

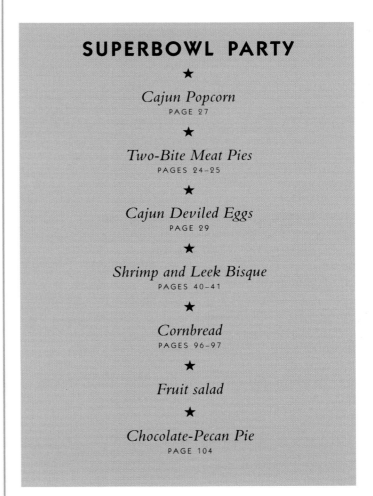

SUPERBOWL PARTY

★

Cajun Popcorn
PAGE 27

★

Two-Bite Meat Pies
PAGES 24–25

★

Cajun Deviled Eggs
PAGE 29

★

Shrimp and Leek Bisque
PAGES 40–41

★

Cornbread
PAGES 96–97

★

Fruit salad

★

Chocolate-Pecan Pie
PAGE 104

YELLOW SQUASH AND POTATO SOUP

A smooth, thick broth is poured over bits of browned potato in this rich, yet inexpensive, soup. If you want to make ahead, refrigerate after pureeing, then reheat and add the cream just before serving.

SERVES 4

2 tbsp. butter
½ cup chopped onion
1 clove garlic, minced
2 baking potatoes, cubed but not peeled
2–3 yellowneck squash, sliced
3 cups poultry stock (page 16) or canned broth
pinch of cayenne
pinch of fresh-ground black pepper
1 tsp. paprika
½ tsp. thyme
½ tsp. basil
salt to taste
¾ cup light cream

≈ In a skillet over medium heat, melt the butter. Saute the onion and garlic until wilted, about 5 minutes. Add the potatoes and saute 8–10 minutes. (You may need to add another tablespoon of butter at this point.) Remove 1 cup potatoes and keep warm. Add the squash to the skillet and saute about 3 minutes.

≈ In a saucepan, mix together the poultry stock and seasonings, then add the sauteed vegetables. Bring to a boil, then reduce the heat and simmer about 40 minutes. Puree the soup in batches in a blender or food processor.

≈ Return the pureed soup to the saucepan and heat through. Add the cream and salt to taste and heat through but do not boil. Divide the reserved potatoes among serving bowls and ladle the soup over the potatoes.

BELOW A long avenue of ancient oaks leads to Oak Alley Plantation, Vacherie, a landmark of antebellum architecture with its Doric columns and two-story colonnaded veranda.

CRAB-CORN CHOWDER

My favorite recipe in this book. The soup has a wonderful rich taste.

SERVES 4

2 tbsp. butter
½ onion, chopped
1 stalk celery, finely chopped
1 clove garlic, minced
1½ cups seafood stock (page 17)
½ cup dry white wine or poultry stock (page 16)
1 cup fresh or frozen corn kernels
¼ tsp. dried thyme
½ tsp. salt
dash of cayenne
¼ tsp. white pepper
1 cup half-and-half
½ cup sour cream
½ lb. crab meat
1 tbsp. chopped fresh parsley
2 green onions, chopped

≈ In a large saucepan over low heat, melt the butter. Saute the onion, celery and garlic until wilted, about 5 minutes.

≈ Add the seafood stock and wine and bring to a boil. Add the corn and spices. Return to a boil, then reduce the heat and simmer, uncovered, about 20 minutes. Stir in the half-and-half and continue simmering for 10 minutes but do not boil. Whisk in the sour cream. Add the crab meat, parsley and green onions, and heat just enough to warm the crab. Do not allow to boil.

CREAM OF ARTICHOKE SOUP

Start with fresh artichoke because this delicious soup uses the water in which the artichokes are cooked for extra flavor. Canned artichokes do not give the same rich flavor.

SERVES 4–6

STOCK

2 large or 3 medium globe artichokes
1 tbsp. lemon juice
½ tsp. salt
2 tbsp. olive oil
2 garlic cloves, crushed

SOUP

2 tbsp. butter
½ cup finely chopped onion
1 cup reserved artichoke cooking water
2 cups chicken stock or canned broth
reserved artichoke scrapings
⅛ tsp. cayenne
2 tbsp. fresh basil
3 tbsp. all-purpose flour
1½ cups heavy cream
reserved sliced artichoke hearts
salt to taste

≈ Cut most of the stem off the artichokes, leaving only a ½-inch stub. Bend the outer petals back until they snap off, leaving the meat at the bottoms of the leaves attached to the heart. Continue snapping off leaves until you've removed several rows, then with a large knife, slice off the remaining artichoke just above the base of the remaining leaves. Collect the discarded leaves and stems in a large bowl or bag.

≈ In a medium saucepan over high heat, bring 1 quart water to a boil. Add the lemon juice, salt, olive oil, garlic and artichoke hearts and simmer until the hearts can be easily pierced with a fork, but are still firm, not mushy, 20–25 minutes.

≈ Remove the hearts from the water and save 1 cup of the cooking water, discarding the rest. When the artichoke hearts are cool enough to handle, use a spoon to scoop the chokes out of the centers. With a sharp knife, trim away the stringy remains of any leaves around the edges. Slice the hearts and set aside.

≈ Place the reserved leaves and stems in a large pot, cover with water and bring to a boil, then lower the heat and simmer 20–25 minutes. Drain and allow the leaves to cool. When they are cool enough to handle, scrape the flesh from the bottoms of the leaves and reserve. Remove the stringy exteriors of the stems and slice the soft insides into a bowl with the leaf scrapings.

≈ In a small skillet over medium heat, melt the butter. Saute the onions until wilted, about 5 minutes. Set aside.

≈ In a medium saucepan, bring the aritchoke cooking water and chicken stock to a boil. Lower the heat and add the artichoke scrapings, cayenne and basil, then simmer 5 minutes.

≈ Mix the flour with a little of the cream and stir until smooth. Whisk the soup until smooth, then whisk in the remaining cream. Bring to just below the boiling point, then add the artichoke slices. Taste and adjust the salt.

CRAWFISH BISQUE

Crawfish Bisque is a very special time-consuming dish, but the results are delicious. The bodies of the crawfish are stuffed with a cornbread stuffing, then cooked in the bisque to absorb the broth. Served over rice, this bisque is a filling main dish. The best part comes at the bottom of the bowl, when the soup is gone and the stuffed crawfish remain. Holding the shell in one hand, scoop out the stuffing with your spoon. Yum!

At a minimum, cook the crawfish, make the stock and bake the cornbread a day in advance – and then plan to spend most of the next day in the kitchen, too.

SERVES 4–6

STOCK

1 large onion, sliced
1 lemon, sliced
2 garlic cloves, crushed
3 fresh parsley sprigs
1 stalk celery, including leaves, sliced
2 whole cloves
1 tbsp. whole mustard seed
1 tsp. celery seed
2 bay leaves
½ tsp. red-pepper flakes
1 tsp. black pepper
1 tsp. salt
5 lbs. whole crawfish

≈ Add all the ingredients, except the crawfish, to a large stockpot of boiling water and boil for 15–20 minutes to develop the flavor, then add the crawfish. Return to a boil, then simmer for 20 minutes. Remove the crawfish with tongs and plunge into cold water. Return the stock to a low heat to simmer while you clean the crawfish.

≈ To clean the crawfish, twist off the tails from the bodies, and cut out all the tail meat. Save the tail meat in 1 bowl. Remove the yellow fat from the bodies and save the fat in a second bowl. Pull the body shells – the thorax – free from the innards, and break off eyes and beaks. Save the best shells for stuffing. Place the innards, any small or broken shells, the heads and the remains of the tail shells in the stock, and continue simmering for total cooking time of 2 hours.

≈ Strain the stock, discarding the vegetables and shells. Reserve 6 cups stock: freeze any leftover stock for future use.

STUFFED CRAWFISH

4–5 crawfish bodies per person
2 tbsp. butter
½ cup chopped onion
¼ cup chopped green onions
¼ cup chopped green pepper
1 rib celery, chopped
2 cloves garlic, minced
1 tbsp. chopped fresh parsley
1 tsp. fresh thyme or ¼ tsp. dried
½ tsp. salt
⅛ tsp. black pepper
few drops of Tabasco sauce
1 tsp. lemon juice
1 egg, lightly beaten
2 cups finely crumbled cornbread (pages 96–97)
½ reserved crawfish tail meat, ground or finely chopped
½ reserved crawfish fat
reserved crawfish stock (see above) to moisten, if necessary

OVEN TEMPERATURE: 350°

≈ Thoroughly clean the crawfish shells, removing any bits of innards that remain. Let dry on paper towels while you prepare stuffing.

≈ In a large skillet, melt the butter over low heat. Saute the onions, green pepper, celery and garlic, 5 minutes. Remove from the heat, and put in a bowl with the remaining ingredients, except the stock. The stuffing should be moist enough that it sticks together when you roll some into a small ball: it should not be mushy. Add some more stock if needed.

≈ Fill the crawfish shells with cornbread mixture, pressing the stuffing so it is solid and not crumbly. Put the stuffed shells on an ungreased baking sheet and bake at 350° for 10 minutes. Remove from oven and set aside.

RIGHT This stately mansion, built in 1830 on the banks of the Bayou Teche, New Iberia, was once the center of a great plantation. Framed by magnolias and ancient live oaks dripping with Spanish moss, Shadows-on-the-Teche is now owned by the National Trust for Historic Preservation.

BISQUE

¼ cup all-purpose flour
¼ cup lard
1 medium tomato, seeded and chopped
1 rib celery, chopped
1 clove garlic, minced
½ cup chopped onion
¼ cup chopped green pepper
6 cups reserved crawfish stock (see above)
½ reserved crawfish tail meat
½ reserved crawfish fat
1 tsp. fresh thyme or ¼ tsp. dried
1 bay leaf
1 tsp. Worcestershire sauce
½ tsp. salt
¼ tsp. black pepper
⅛ tsp. cayenne
1 tsp. fresh-squeezed lemon juice
reserved stuffed crawfish shells (see above)
3 cups cooked rice to serve
½ cup chopped green onions

≈ Make a dark, mahogany-colored roux of lard and flour (page 15). Remove from heat and stir in the tomato, celery, garlic, onion and green pepper. Return to very low heat and cook until vegetables are limp, about 5 minutes. Set aside.

≈ In a large pot, bring the crawfish stock to a boil. Add the roux and vegetables to the stock 1 spoonful at a time, whisking to mix thoroughly. Add the crawfish tail meat, fat, seasonings and lemon juice. Gently, with tongs or large spoon, add the stuffed shells to soup. Simmer 45 minutes, uncovered.

≈ Put rice in bottom of each bowl. Fish out the stuffed shells and divide among the bowls. Add the green onions to the soup, then ladle the bisque into the bowls.

CRAWFISH BISQUE

GUMBOS AND JAMBALAYAS

—★—

CHICKEN AND ANDOUILLE SAUSAGE GUMBO

The spicy flavor of this roux-based gumbo comes from the Andouille sausage and the seasonings in the chicken. Taste before serving and adjust seasonings.

SERVES 6

¼ cup all-purpose flour
1 tsp. salt
½ tsp. black pepper
¼ tsp. cayenne
1 tsp. paprika
½ tsp. onion powder
½ tsp. garlic powder
3 whole or 6 half uncooked chicken breasts, skinned and cubed
¼ cup vegetable oil
1 cup all-purpose flour
1 cup lard
2 cups chopped onion
1½ cups chopped green pepper
1½ cups chopped celery
2 qts. poultry stock (page 16)
¾ lb. Andouille sausage, cubed
2 garlic cloves, minced
3 cups cooked rice to serve

≈ Mix ¼ cup flour with the seasonings in a small bowl, then toss the chicken until the cubes are well coated with spices. Heat the oil in a large skillet and saute the chicken until browned. Drain on paper towels, if necessary. Set aside.

≈ Combine the 1 cup flour and lard to make a dark, mahogany-colored roux (page 15). Remove the roux from the heat and add the chopped vegetables. Stir until the roux stops darkening. Return to the heat and cook until the vegetables are limp, about 5 minutes.

≈ Add the poultry stock, a little at a time, stirring until well blended. Bring to a boil, then add the chicken, Andouille and garlic. Reduce the heat and simmer for 1 hour. You may wish to skim the gumbo occasionally if fat from the roux or the sausage rises to the top. Taste and adjust seasonings. Serve over rice.

GUMBO

MUCH OF THE HISTORY OF CAJUNS AND THEIR COOKING IS MIXED into the stew they call gumbo. Like many types of Louisiana food, gumbo traces its lineage to a French dish, bouillabaise, a fish stew. The name gumbo is derived from the word "kingombo," a type of okra, the seeds of which Africans brought with them on slave ships. Filé, powdered sassafras leaves that are used as a seasoning and a thickener, was contributed by the Choctaw Indians. Spanish settlers added red peppers. And instead of Mediterranean fish, lobster and eels, Gulf fishermen used shrimp, crab and oysters.

≈ Almost any kind of meat, fish or game can be used in gumbo: roast beef, alligator, frogs' legs, hot links or other sausages, eggs and dried shrimp are some of the more unusual ingredients. More common are shrimp, crab, oysters, crawfish, redfish, chicken, duck and spicy Andouille sausage.

≈ Most gumbos begin with roux, a slow-cooked mixture of lard and flour that adds flavor, color and body to the stew. Then come chopped vegetables – and a rich stock, simmered most of the day from shrimp shells, crab carcasses or chicken parts. Gumbo is spicy, although not as hot as its cousin, jambalaya.

≈ Okra can also be used to thicken gumbo, and health-conscious people use it instead of roux. Filé powder is another thickener that is added only after the gumbo has finished cooking and is removed from the heat, or is sprinkled into serving bowls. Cooking the filé powder gives it an unpleasant flavor, and it will turn gumbo dark and stringy.

≈ Gumbo is ladled over cooked white rice in wide, shallow bowls.

SEAFOOD GUMBO WITH OKRA

Okra is used as the thickener, so this gumbo is lighter than a roux-based gumbo. It is only mildly spicy. Use at least three different type of fish and shellfish, in whatever combination of fresh seafood is available: shrimp, crab, oysters, frogs' legs, crawfish tails, clams, mussels, scallops, or fileted redfish, red snapper, cod or other fish, cut into cubes.

SERVES 8

2 tbsp. vegetable oil
2 cups chopped onion
1½ cups chopped green pepper
1 cup chopped celery
3 garlic cloves, minced
3 large or 4 medium tomatoes, seeded and chopped
8-oz. can tomato sauce
2 qts. seafood stock (page 17)
1 tbsp. fresh-squeezed lemon juice
2 bay leaves
1 tbsp. fresh thyme or 1 tsp. dried
1 tsp. salt
¼ tsp. black pepper
⅛ tsp. cayenne
⅛ tsp. white pepper
½ tsp. paprika
1½ lbs. okra, thawed and well drained if frozen, sliced
2 lbs. mixed seafood (see introduction)
4 cups cooked rice to serve
filé powder, optional

≈ In a large skillet, heat the oil. Saute the onion, pepper, celery and garlic until limp, about 5 minutes. Transfer to a large saucepan or stockpot and add the tomatoes, tomato sauce, seafood stock, lemon juice and seasonings. Bring to a boil, then reduce the heat and simmer, uncovered, 5 minutes.

≈ Add the okra and return to a boil, then reduce the heat and simmer 30 minutes. Add the seafood: cubed fish and frogs' legs take the longest times to cook, oysters the least.

≈ Spoon the rice into individual large bowls. Ladle the gumbo over the rice. If desired, add a pinch of filé powder to each bowl.

CHICKEN, ANDOUILLE AND SHRIMP JAMBALAYA

CASUAL DINNER PARTY

★

Cajun BBQ Shrimp with lots of French bread
PAGES 30–31

★

Green salad

★

Chicken and Andouille Sausage Gumbo
PAGE 47

★

Sweet-Potato and Pecan Pie
PAGE 105

ABOVE The Afton Villa Gardens lie just north of St. Francisville, which is located 35 miles north of Baton Rouge on the Mississippi River. The gardens were once part of a plantation on which stood a beautiful French Gothic-style villa, built in the mid-1800s. The villa survived the Civil War only to burn down in the 1960s.

DUCK, OYSTER AND ARTICHOKE GUMBO

The delicate flavors of duck, oysters and artichokes are combined in this roux-based gumbo. It is a two-day job to roast the duck and make stock, then to make the gumbo, but the product of all that time and effort is a rich and hearty stew.

SERVES 8

1 domestic duck
½ cup lard
½ cup all-purpose flour
1 cup chopped onion
1 cup chopped green pepper
1 cup chopped celery
2 cloves garlic
8 cups duck stock (see below)
about 2 cups reserved cooked duck meat
1 tbsp. fresh basil or 1 tsp. dried
½ tsp. dry mustard
1 tsp. salt
½ tsp. black pepper
¼ tsp. cayenne
1 tsp. paprika
1½ tsp. fresh thyme or ½ tsp. dried
4 artichoke hearts, cooked and sliced (see Cream of Artichoke Soup, page 43)
1 dozen oysters, shucked and cut into bite-size pieces
½ cup chopped green onions
¼ cup chopped fresh parsley
4 cups cooked rice to serve

≈ Roast the duck as directed on pages 70–71, omitting the onion, spice and orange juice mixture. Cut the meat from the bones, chop and refrigerate the meat: you will need about 2 cups meat for this recipe. Make a stock from the carcass as directed on page 16.

≈ In a medium saucepan, make a dark, mahogany-colored roux of lard and flour (page 15). Remove from the heat and add the onion, pepper, celery and garlic. Stir until the roux stops darkening. Return to the heat and cook until the vegetables are limp, about 5 minutes.

≈ In large saucepan or stockpot, bring the duck stock to a boil. Add the roux, 1 large spoonful at a time, whisking after each addition until well blended. Add the duck meat and seasonings, then simmer 40 minutes. Add the artichokes and simmer 5 minutes more. Add the oysters, green onions and parsley, and cook until the edges of the oysters start to curl, 2–3 minutes. Spoon the rice into large individual bowls. Ladle the gumbo over the rice.

CHICKEN, ANDOUILLE AND SHRIMP JAMBALAYA

All the spiciness in this jambalaya comes from the meat. Be sure to taste before you serve, and adjust seasonings, especially if you've had to substitute other ham or sausage for the Tasso and Andouille. This level is what I call base-line spiciness. It's hot to most people, but not as spicy as traditional Cajun cooking, so add more black and cayenne pepper if you like mouth-searing food.

SERVES 6–8

1 tsp. salt
½ tsp. cayenne
½ tsp. black pepper
1½ tsp. fresh thyme or ½ tsp. dried
1 whole or 2 half uncooked chicken breasts, skinned and cubed
2 tbsp. vegetable oil
1½ cups chopped celery
1½ cups chopped onion
1½ cups chopped green pepper
2 garlic cloves, minced
4 oz. Tasso or other smoked ham, chopped
6 oz. Andouille or other spicy sausage, sliced
1 lb. tomatoes, seeded and chopped
8-oz. can tomato sauce
1 cup poultry or seafood stock (pages 16–17)
½ lb. medium shrimp, shelled and deveined
½ cup chopped green onions
about 5 cups cooked rice to serve

≈ In a small bowl, mix together the salt, cayenne, black pepper and thyme. Toss the chicken, until it is well coated with spices.

≈ In a large skillet or Dutch oven, heat the oil. Saute the chicken, stirring almost constantly, until the chicken is browned, 6–8 minutes. Add the celery, onion, green pepper and garlic, and saute until the vegetables are limp, about 5 minutes.

≈ Add the Tasso, Andouille sausage, tomatoes, tomato sauce and stock and stir and cook until mixture is bubbling. Reduce the heat and simmer until tomatoes have cooked down and liquid is slightly reduced, creating a rich, red broth. Add the shrimp and cook until the shrimp are opaque and tightly curled, 2–3 minutes. Taste and adjust the seasonings. It should be very spicy. Add the green onions and enough rice so that the mixture is neither soupy nor dry.

NOTE:

≈ If you did not cook the rice with salt, you will need to increase the amount of salt in the jambalaya.

SEAFOOD JAMBALAYA

Jambalaya is traditionally made with ham, but it's not a necessity. I made this jambalaya for a friend who doesn't eat meat. You may add ham back in, if you desire – ¼–½ lb. chopped ham – and if you use Tasso ham, you may need to decrease the seasonings.

SERVES 6–8

2 tbsp. vegetable oil
1 onion, chopped
1 green pepper, chopped
2 ribs celery, chopped
3 cloves garlic, minced
3 large tomatoes, seeded and chopped
8-oz. can tomato sauce
1 cup seafood stock (page 17)
¼ cup chopped fresh parsley
2 bay leaves
1 tbsp. fresh thyme or 1 tsp. dried
1 tsp. salt
¼ tsp. black pepper
½ tsp. cayenne
⅛ tsp. white pepper
2 lbs. fresh shrimp, crab meat, crawfish or oysters, or any combination, prepared
½ cup chopped green onions
4 cups cooked rice to serve

≈ In a deep skillet or Dutch oven, heat the oil. Saute the onion, green pepper, celery and garlic until vegetables are limp, about 5 minutes. Add the tomatoes, tomato sauce, stock, parsley and seasonings and simmer gently until the tomatoes are cooked down and some of the liquids have reduced. Taste and adjust the seasonings.

≈ Add the seafood. (If using oysters, cut into bite-size pieces and add in the last 2–3 minutes of cooking.) Simmer just until the shrimp are opaque and tightly curled, 5–7 minutes. Just before serving, mix in the green onions. Serve over the rice.

NOTE:

≈ If the rice is not cooked with salt, you will need additional salt in the jambalaya.

JAMBALAYA

THERE ARE ALL SORTS OF THEORIES ABOUT THE ORIGIN OF THE word jambalaya, but the most common one is that it comes from the Spanish word jamon, meaning ham, or the French word jambon, also meaning ham. So it's not surprising that virtually all jambalaya recipes include at least a little ham, even if it is (horrors!) turkey ham.

≈ Jambalaya is a descendant of Spanish paella, which was brought to Louisiana during the Spanish occupation of the late 18th century. But instead of the saffron that colors paella a golden yellow, Cajuns use cayenne to season jambalaya.

≈ Jambalaya is a sort of hash. There are some requisite ingredients – rice, spices, a little ham, lots of tomatoes, onions, celery and bell peppers – but other additions can be any meat or seafood leftovers in your refrigerator. Most common are shellfish, chicken, and sausage, but just about anything else is acceptable, from spareribs to rabbit to alligator.

≈ Most jambalaya is made on the stovetop, but once the vegetables are sauteed and the liquids are hot, it can be mounded into a large casserole dish and baked. Many recipes call for uncooked rice to be added while the jambalaya is still sloshing with liquids, but I prefer to add cooked rice until I get just the texture and consistency I want. Otherwise, if there's just a little less liquid than you think, the rice can absorb it all and still be slightly crunchy, while you're left with a dry jambalaya.

RIGHT *While New Orleans is the urban center of Louisiana, the capitol sits to the north at Baton Rouge on the Mississippi River, surrounded by 27 acres of formal gardens.*

SEAFOOD

★

CRAWFISH PIE

Paprika colors the rich-and-creamy filling pink in this recipe. If you can find crawfish tails already peeled and cooked, buy them. You're in for a lot of work if you have to cook and clean enough whole crawfish to produce enough tail meat for this recipe. Use your favorite piecrust recipe, or the one for Two-Bite Meat Pies (page 24).

SERVES 6–8

¼ cup lard
¼ cup all-purpose flour
½ cup chopped onion
½ cup chopped celery
½ cup chopped green pepper
2 garlic cloves, minced
2 tbsp. chopped fresh parsley
½ cup seafood stock (page 17) or clam juice
1½ cups half-and-half
1 tsp. paprika
¾ tsp. fresh thyme or ¼ tsp. dried
1½ tsp. chopped fresh basil or ½ tsp. dried
¼ tsp. black pepper
¼ tsp. cayenne
⅛ tsp. white pepper
1 tsp. salt
2 tsp. fresh-squeezed lemon juice
1½ lbs. crawfish tails, shelled and cooked
¾ cup chopped green onions
pastry dough for 2-crust pie

OVEN TEMPERATURE: 375°

≈ In a heavy saucepan, make a peanut-butter-colored roux of lard and flour (page 15). Remove from the heat, add the vegetables, garlic and parsley. Return to the heat, and cook until the vegetables are wilted, about 5 minutes.

≈ In another pan, heat the seafood stock and half-and-half to a slow boil. Whisk in the roux, 1 large spoonful at a time, whisking after each addition. Add the seasonings and lemon juice and bring to a boil, then reduce the heat and simmer for 20 minutes. Add the crawfish tails and green onions. Taste and adjust the seasonings, then let cool to lukewarm.

≈ Roll out the piecrust dough and line a 9-inch pie plate with half the dough, sprinkling a little flour over the bottom to prevent sogginess. Add filling and top with the second crust. Trim and seal the edges, pinching into a fluted edge.

≈ Bake at 375° until the crust is golden brown, about 30 minutes. Let cool about 10 minutes before serving.

BLACKENED REDFISH

The sudden and huge popularity of blackened redfish in the mid-1980s created a shortage of redfish, especially outside the South. Fortunately, this recipe can be used with many other types of fish, as long as they have strong connective tissue and are no thicker than ¾ inch. Red snapper, tilefish, grouper, pompano, salmon and catfish fillets all work well. Most recently, I used a New Zealand sea bass that was delicious.

≈ This method uses an extremely hot skillet and will set off your smoke alarm. Open a window, turn on the ventilation system and keep a tight-fitting lid close at hand to smother any flame-ups – they are common. For that reason, don't try this if you have an above-stove microwave oven. You must use a cast-iron skillet: the high temperature will ruin any other. A charcoal barbecue will not get the pan hot enough.

≈ In spite of all these warnings and instructions, blackened fish is an easy and quick dish, and the results are delicious. I recommend getting one small, extra fillet the first time you try this, and experimenting with it, just to get a feel for the method.

≈ This dish requires all your attention. You may want to have an extra pair of hands in the kitchen to make side dishes and the butter sauce just before serving. Otherwise, make your side dishes and butter sauce before you begin cooking, then reheat the sauce (preferably in a microwave) to melt the butter at serving time.

≈ Use onion and garlic powder and dried herbs instead of fresh in this recipe because the high cooking temperature gives fresh herbs and garlic an unpleasant burned taste. The fish can be from 4–12 oz. each, depending on appetites, but no more than ¾ inches thick, and the more uniform the thickness, the better.

SERVES 6

6 fish fillets
¾ cup (1½ sticks) unsalted butter, melted

SEASONING MIX:

1½ tsp. salt
1 tbsp. paprika
1 tsp. onion powder
1 tsp. garlic powder
1 tsp. dried thyme
½ tsp. dried oregano
½ tsp. black pepper
1 tsp. cayenne

BUTTER SAUCE:

½ cup (1 stick) unsalted butter, melted
1 tbsp. fresh-squeezed lemon juice
1 green onion, finely minced
¼ tsp. cayenne
¼ tsp. salt

≈ Put a cast-iron skillet over high heat and heat until the pan begins to smoke and white ash forms on the bottom, at least 10 minutes. If after 20 minutes, there is no ash, your stove may not produce enough heat. Sprinkle a few drops of water in the pan. If they dance, the skillet is hot enough to do the job, but cooking may take an extra 30 seconds a side.

≈ Combine all the ingredients for the seasoning mix and set aside.

≈ Combine all the ingredients for the butter sauce and set aside.

≈ Dip the fillets in plain melted unsalted butter, then sprinkle the seasoning mix on both sides and pat into the butter. The butter will congeal on the cold fish and may flake off. If it does, put it in pan with the barest side up and spoon some melted butter over the bare spots. But be wary: the butter is likely to flame up during cooking. If it does, put a lid on the skillet to smother the fire, then continue.

≈ When the pan is ready, put 2 fillets in, moving quickly and cook until the bottoms are blackened, up to 2 minutes. (The fish will not be solid black, but ridges, edges and grains of seasonings will be blackened.) Turn over. If the thickness is not uniform, you may wish to press down gently with pancake turner during cooking. Again, cook until ridges on bottom are blackened, up to 2 minutes. The interior of the fish should be opaque but juicy. Keep warm in a low oven while you repeat with the remaining fillets.

≈ Reheat the butter sauce if necessary and pour over the fish. Serve at once.

PECAN CATFISH

PECAN CATFISH

Instead of flour or cornmeal, these easy-to-prepare catfish fillets are baked in a ground-pecan coating. The flavor is deliciously set off by sour cream, mustard and green onions.

SERVES 4

¼ cup Dijon-style mustard
¼ cup sour cream
2 tbsp. milk
½ cup finely chopped green onions
1 cup finely ground pecans
4 catfish fillets, skinned, about 6 oz. each

OVEN TEMPERATURE: 500°

≈ In a large, shallow bowl, mix together the mustard, sour cream, milk and green onions. Dip the catfish fillets in the mustard mixture: the mixture is a little thick, so you may need to spread some on any bare spots. Carefully dredge the fillets in the ground pecans.

≈ Place the catfish fillets on a greased baking sheet and bake at 500° until fish is opaque but still juicy, 8–10 minutes.

SUMMER DINNER PARTY

★

Hot Crab Spread with crackers and crudites
PAGES 28–29

Cold Shrimp in Horseradish Sauce
PAGE 30

Corn Salad
PAGE 34

Spicy Green Beans
PAGE 91

Cornbread
PAGES 96–97

Pecan Catfish
PAGES 58–59

Peach-Amaretto Ice Cream
PAGE 109

FRIED CATFISH

Catfish are cheap and plentiful in the United States, especially since they are now raised on commercial catfish farms. These fillets are quartered, so the thickest parts are on the edges and they cook more evenly. They are deep-fried, but if you prefer, you can pan-fry them, as long as you cook them a little longer. Serve the fillets with lemon wedges and Tartar Sauce (page 121), accompanied by Hushpuppies (page 95) and Coleslaw (page 35) or Corn Salad (page 34).

SERVES 4

½ cup all-purpose flour
½ tsp. salt
½ tsp. black pepper
⅛ tsp. cayenne
½ tsp. paprika
1 tsp. dry mustard
1 egg, lightly beaten
¾ cup milk
few drops of Tabasco sauce
¾ cup cornmeal
¼ cup corn flour
¼ cup all-purpose flour
½ tsp. salt
½ tsp. black pepper
½ tsp. cayenne
½ tsp. onion powder
½ tsp. garlic powder
4 catfish fillets, about 6 oz. each, skinned and quartered
vegetable oil for frying

≈ Set out 3 bowls. In the first bowl, combine the all-purpose flour, salt, pepper, cayenne, paprika and dry mustard. In the second bowl, mix the egg and milk together and add a few drops of Tabasco sauce. In the third bowl, combine the cornmeal and remaining ingredients, except the catfish and oil.

≈ Dip the catfish pieces first in the flour mixture, then shake off the excess. Next, dip the catfish in the egg mixture, then in the cornmeal mixture, again shaking off the excess. (You may also put the 2 breading mixtures in paper or plastic bags, and shake the catfish in the bags to coat.)

≈ In deep skillet or wok, heat 3 inches of oil to 350°. Add a few pieces of breaded catfish, making sure you don't crowd them and cook until golden brown, turning once, 1½–2 minutes a side. Drain well on paper towels and keep warm in the oven while you fry the remaining catfish. Make sure the oil returns to 350° before frying the next batch.

ALMOND TROUT

The classic method for preparing this dish is to coat the trout with flour or bread crumbs, then pan-fry them. I prefer to broil my trout with just a little olive oil and paprika, then add the crunchy topping of almonds and green onions. The result is a simpler dish with a wonderful flavor that saves a few calories.

SERVES 2

2 small trout, about 1½ lbs. each, filleted with the heads removed (can be whole or in 2 pieces)
2 tbsp. olive oil
½ tsp. paprika
3 tbsp. butter
½ cup sliced blanched almonds
1 tsp. Worcestershire sauce
2 tsp. fresh-squeezed lemon juice
1 tsp. grated lemon peel
few drops of Tabasco sauce
3 green onions, chopped
2 tbsp. chopped fresh parsley

Spray a broiler pan with a non-stick spray. Put the trout on the rack, skin side down. Combine the olive oil and paprika, and brush over filleted meat. Put under the broiler, about 5 inches from the heat, and broil unskinned side up until opaque but still juicy, 5–6 minutes, using a rule of 10 minutes per inch of the fillet's thickness.

≈ While fish is cooking, in a small skillet, melt the butter. Add the almonds and cook until they are a golden brown. Add the Worcestershire sauce, lemon juice, lemon peel and Tabasco sauce and mix well. Remove from the heat, add the green onions and parsley, and quickly spoon over the broiled trout.

GRILLED SHARK

This barbecue recipe is an easy and tasty way to cook shark, or other dense-fleshed fish such as swordfish. I think it is delicious plain, but you can also serve it with dilled Butter Sauce for Fish (page 124.)

SERVES 4

3 tbsp. fresh-squeezed lemon juice
3 tbsp. fresh-squeezed lime juice
½ tsp. grated lemon peel
½ tsp. grated lime peel
¼ cup olive oil
¼ cup chopped fresh dill
3 garlic cloves, minced
pinch of salt
4 shark steaks, about 6 oz. each
fresh-ground black pepper

≈ In a glass or other non-reactive dish, combine all the ingredients, except the shark and pepper. Place the shark steaks in the marinade, turning to coat thoroughly, and spreading dill and garlic bits over tops of the fish. Sprinkle with fresh-ground black pepper, cover with plastic wrap and refrigerate about 2 hours, turning once or twice.

≈ When the barbecue coals have stopped flaming, place the shark steaks on a lightly greased grill. Cook about 5 minutes each side, turning once. (Total cooking time should be about 10 minutes per inch of thickness.) Baste with the extra marinade, if desired. The fish is cooked through when the flesh turns opaque, but is still juicy.

CRAB-STUFFED FISH

Use whole trout, pompano, flounder or sole for this dish, cooked for individual servings if you use small fish. Or, present an elegant platter of a large, stuffed fish surrounded by lemon slices and parsley sprigs. Fresh crab meat is best but frozen or canned are acceptable. If you wish, serve with Butter Sauce for Fish (page 124.)

SERVES 4

2 tbsp. butter
6 green onions, chopped
1½ cups coarsely chopped mushrooms
1 tbsp. chopped fresh parsley
1 clove garlic, minced
¼ tsp. salt
¼ tsp. paprika
¼ tsp. black pepper
2 tbsp. grated Parmesan cheese
¼ cup light or heavy cream
½ lb. fresh crab meat, picked over
4 whole fish, about ½ lb. each, cleaned and boned
salt to taste
fresh-ground black pepper to taste
flour for dredging (optional)
olive oil or melted butter

OVEN TEMPERATURE: 350°

≈ In a small skillet, melt the butter. Saute the onions, mushrooms, parsley and garlic until limp, about 5 minutes. Stir in the salt, paprika, pepper, Parmesan, and cream until well mixed. Add the crab, stirring gently. Set aside.

≈ Rinse the fish and pat dry with paper towels. Season the insides lightly with salt and pepper. You may dredge the trout in flour at this point, covering the outside only with a thin coat of flour, and shaking off excess. The flouring step is optional.

≈ Stuff with the crab mixture, then skewer the fish closed with toothpicks, or sew a few large stitches with coarse thread. Put the fish in a lightly oiled baking pan and brush with olive oil or drizzle with melted butter.

≈ Bake the fish at 350° until the flesh at thickest point is opaque but is still juicy, about 10 minutes. Do not wait for the fish to flake easily, because it continues cooking after it is removed from the oven, and would be overcooked by the time you serve it.

NOTE:

≈ If you use one large fish, a 2½–3 lb. fish will serve 4–5 people.

CRAWFISH ETOUFFEE

Etouffée means "smothered" in French, and here a rich, spicy roux-based sauce smothers the crawfish. The sauce can be made ahead of time, then reheated and the crawfish added just before serving.

SERVES 4–6

½ cup lard
½ cup all-purpose flour
1 cup chopped onion
1 cup chopped green pepper
½ cup chopped celery
4 cloves garlic, minced
4 medium tomatoes, seeded and chopped
½ cup chopped fresh parsley
2 cups seafood stock (page 17)
½ tsp. cayenne
½ tsp. black pepper
1 tsp. salt
1½ tsp. black pepper
1 tsp. salt
1½ tsp. fresh thyme or ½ tsp. dried
1½ lbs. crawfish tails, shelled and cooked
1 cup chopped green onions
2–3 cups cooked rice to serve

≈ In a heavy saucepan, make a mahogany-colored roux of the lard and flour (page 15.) Remove from the heat, stir in the vegetables and parsley. Return to the heat and cook until the vegetables are limp, about 5 minutes.

≈ In large saucepan, bring the seafood stock to a slow boil. Add the roux and vegetables, 1 spoonful at a time, whisking after each addition until the mixture is smooth. Add the seasoning. Reduce the heat and simmer for 30 minutes.

≈ Add the crawfish tails and simmer until crawfish is heated through, about 5 minutes. Just before serving, stir in the green onions. Serve over rice.

CRAWFISH ETOUFFEE

SHRIMP CREOLE

Whenever possible, start with whole shrimp and use the shrimp heads and shells to make a rich seafood stock for this dish. You can make the sauce ahead of time, then reheat and add shrimp just before serving. This recipe is only mildly spicy, so add more cayenne or Tabasco sauce if you want a fiery dish.

SERVES 6

2 tbsp. vegetable oil
1 cup chopped onion, divided
1 cup chopped green pepper
¾ cup chopped celery
3 garlic cloves, minced
2½ cups fresh tomatoes, seeded and chopped
8-oz. can tomato sauce
½ cup dry red wine or seafood stock (page 17)
1½ cup seafood stock (page 17)
1 tsp. salt
2 bay leaves
2 tbsp. chopped fresh parsley
1 tbsp. chopped fresh basil or 1 tsp. dried
1½ tsp. fresh thyme or ½ tsp. dried
½ tsp. black pepper
¼ tsp. cayenne
few drops of Tabasco sauce
1 tbsp. fresh-squeezed lemon juice
1 lb. medium shrimp, shelled and deveined
¾ cup chopped green onion
3 cups cooked rice to serve

≈ In a large saucepan, heat the oil. Saute ½ cup onions until golden. Add the remaining onions, green pepper, celery and garlic, and saute until vegetables are limp, about 5 minutes.

≈ Add the tomatoes, tomato sauce, wine, stock, seasonings, Tabasco sauce and lemon juice. Bring to a boil, stir well, then reduce the heat and simmer 30 minutes.

≈ Just before serving, add the shrimp and green onions, and cook just until shrimp are opaque and tightly curled, 5–7 minutes. Serve over rice.

LIME-GRILLED SHRIMP

Light on fat and heavy on flavor, this is an easy and delicious barbecue recipe.

SERVES 6

½ cup peanut oil
¼ cup fresh-squeezed lime juice
4 garlic cloves, minced
2 tbsp. chopped fresh cilantro
½ tsp. red-pepper flakes
½ tsp. salt
¼ tsp. black pepper
1½ lbs. medium shrimp, shelled and deveined

≈ In a glass or another non-reactive bowl, mix together all the ingredients, except the shrimp, until well combined. Add the shrimp, turning to make sure each is thoroughly coated, then refrigerate for several hours, turning once or twice. If you're using wooden skewers, soak the skewers in water for at least 1 hour while shrimp are marinating. This helps prevent the skewers burning.

≈ Thread the shrimp on the skewers: the shrimp should not touch each other. When the coals have stopped flaming, place the skewers on the grill, directly over the coals. Cook just until shrimp are opaque and tightly curled, 2–3 minutes a side, turning once. Don't overcook or the shrimp will toughen.

BOILED SHRIMP

Here is a basic recipe for cooking shrimp that are to be eaten cold with a dip, rémoulade sauce or in a salad. Whether you shell them before you cook them is a matter of personal preference. If you like, you can also use wine or beer as the cooking liquid, and you can increase the amount of chili flakes if you like your shrimp spicy.

MAKES 1 LB.

2 carrots, sliced
1 onion, sliced
2 cloves garlic, crushed
1 bay leaf
parsley sprigs
1 tsp. salt
1 tbsp. whole mustard seed
1 tsp. black pepper
¼ tsp. dried chili flakes
1 lemon, sliced
1 lb. shrimp

≈ In a large saucepan, bring 3 quarts water to a boil. Add the carrots, onion, garlic, bay leaf and parsley and continue boiling about 10 minutes to release the vegetables' flavors into the cooking liquid. Add the spices and lemon and boil for another 2 minutes.

≈ Add the shrimp and boil just until the shrimp are opaque and tightly curled, 2–3 minutes. Do not overcook or the shrimp will become tough. Drain and refrigerate, or put on ice.

THE FLAVOR OF NEW ORLEANS

LEFT The Old Absinthe House, located among the burlesque clubs of Bourbon Street, is named for the licorice-flavored green spirit it served before absinthe was banned in the United States.

ABOVE This streetcar named Desire, a namesake of the Tennessee Williams play set in New Orleans, sits in the French Quarter.

RIGHT New Orleans is famous for the elaborate iron grillwork of its balconies.

TOP Like Louisiana's food, its music is a blend of competing cultural strains. New Orleans jazz emerged from Dixieland, rhythm and blues, African drums, Caribbean calypso and gospel choirs. Its landmarks include the clubs of Bourbon Street and Preservation Hall, the city's best-known jazz club.

RIGHT The Pontalba Apartments in New Orleans' French Quarter were built in 1850 and are believed to be the oldest apartment buildings in America. The four-story, red-brick buildings are still such a prestigious address that there is a lengthy waiting list for vacancies.

MEAT AND POULTRY

MUSTARD-BAKED CHICKEN

Coated with a sauce of mustard and sour cream, this chicken dish is easy and tasty.

SERVES 6-8

½ cup sour cream
¼ cup Creole mustard
3 cups finely crumbled cornbread (pages 96–97)
1½ tsp. fresh thyme or ½ tsp. dried
1 tsp. salt
¼ tsp. black pepper
¼ tsp. cayenne
2 chickens, about 2½–3 lbs. each, cut into serving pieces
⅓ cup butter, melted

OVEN TEMPERATURE: 375°

≈ In a small bowl, combine the sour cream and mustard. In another small bowl, mix together the cornbread crumbs and seasonings.

≈ Spread the mustard mixture over the chicken pieces, then roll the chicken in the crumb mixture. Arrange the chicken in a single layer in large, shallow baking dish and drizzle with the melted butter. Bake at 375° until the chicken is golden brown and the juices run clear if tested with the tip of a knife, about 1 hour.

BAKED VEAL CHOPS WITH RICE AND SHRIMP STUFFING

This flavorful dish has a lot of steps, but is not difficult to make.

SERVES 4

STUFFING

1 tbsp. butter
¼ cup chopped onion
1 clove garlic, minced
2 cups beef stock (page 16) or canned broth
½ tsp. grated lemon peel
½ tsp. salt
¼ tsp. black pepper
1½ tsp. fresh thyme or ½ tsp. dried
¾ cup brown rice
¼ cup wild rice
2 tbsp. butter
¼ cup chopped green pepper
¼ cup chopped celery
½ cup chopped green onions
6 oz. shrimp, cooked, shelled, deveined and coarsely chopped

≈ In a small skillet over medium heat, melt the butter. Saute the onion and garlic until limp, about 5 minutes.

≈ In medium saucepan, bring the beef stock to a boil. Add the sauteed onion and garlic, lemon peel, salt, pepper, thyme and rices. Return to a boil, then cover and cook very low until all liquid is absorbed, about 50 minutes.

≈ In skillet over medium heat, melt 2 tablespoons butter. Saute the green pepper and celery until limp, about 5 minutes. Add the green onions and saute 1 minute longer. Add the vegetables and shrimp to the rice, and set aside.

VEAL CHOPS

4 thick veal chops, each at least ¾–1 in. thick
½ cup all-purpose flour
½ tsp. salt
⅛ tsp. pepper
¼ tsp. paprika
¼ tsp. onion powder
¼ tsp. garlic powder
3-4 tbsp. vegetable oil
½-1 cup beef stock (page 16) or canned broth

OVEN TEMPERATURE 350°

≈ Cut a gash on the side of each veal chop, to make a pocket.

≈ Mix together the flour and seasonings in a bowl or paper sack. Dip the chops in the flour.

≈ In a large skillet over high heat, heat the oil. Add the chops and cook until lightly browned on each side, then remove from heat.

≈ Spoon some rice stuffing into the pocket of each veal chop. Place the chops in a shallow baking pan and pour in enough beef stock to cover the bottom of the pan by ¼ inch. Cover the pan and bake at 350° until meat is tender and all traces of pink are gone, about 1 hour. Serve extra stuffing on side.

ROAST DUCK

Because domestic ducks are so fatty, I roast them unstuffed so the fat that cooks out doesn't overpower the taste of the stuffing. Serve this duck with Baked Crawfish-Cornbread Stuffing (page 97) on the side, or use the meat in Duck With Shrimp and Fettucine (page 81), a duck salad or Duck Rice (page 77).

SERVES 4

1 domestic duck, about 4–5 lb.
1 tsp. salt
½ tsp. black pepper
1 tsp. dry mustard
1 tsp. garlic powder
½ tsp. dried sage
1 onion, quartered
2 tbsp. vegetable oil
1 onion, chopped
2 cloves garlic, minced
1 stalk celery, minced
1 bay leaf
2 tbsp. Worcestershire sauce
½ cup orange juice

OVEN TEMPERATURE: 350°

≈ Remove the neck and organs from cavity of the duck, and save for another use. Mix together the spices in a small bowl. Rub the duck inside and out with the spice mixture. Put the quartered onion in cavity, to draw any off-flavors, then put the duck on rack in a roasting pan, to allow fat to drain off.

≈ In a skillet over medium heat, heat the oil. Saute the chopped onion, garlic, celery and bay leaf until the vegetables are wilted, about 5 minutes. Add the Worcestershire sauce and orange juice, and heat just until mixture comes to boil. Pour over the duck.

≈ Roast the duck at 350° for 20 minutes per pound, basting occasionally with pan juices.

ROAST DUCK

CREOLE CHICKEN STEW WITH DUMPLINGS

This chicken stew in a spicy tomato sauce takes the better part of a day, but it makes a hearty dish that is worth the effort. It begins with a chicken stock, made with the chicken that eventually goes into the stew.

SERVES 4

CHICKEN STOCK

1 chicken, about 3½ lbs., cut in half
2 lbs. extra chicken necks and backs
2 carrots, unpeeled, cut into chunks
½ onion, cut into chunks
2 stalks celery, including leaves, sliced
1 bay leaf
1½ tsp. fresh thyme or ½ tsp. dried
4 black peppercorns
1 tsp. salt

≈ Put all ingredients into a large stockpot and cover with water. Bring to a boil and skim off the gray-brown foam. Reduce the heat and simmer about 45 minutes. Remove the chicken halves and let cool briefly so you can handle them. Cut the meat from bones and refrigerate the meat. Return the bones and skin to stock and continue simmering, uncovered, for a total of about 3 hours. Strain the stock, discarding the bones and vegetables. You will need 5 cups of stock for the Creole stew; freeze or refrigerate any remaining stock for future use. Skim any fat from the top of the stock.

STEW

3 tbsp. lard
3 tbsp. all-purpose flour
1½ cups chopped onion
1 cup chopped green pepper
1 cup chopped celery
2 medium tomatoes, seeded and chopped
5 cups chicken stock (above)
meat from 1 chicken, cut into strips or bite-size pieces
¼ tsp. dry mustard
½ tsp. paprika
⅛ tsp. white pepper
⅛ tsp. cayenne
salt to taste
2 tbsp. chopped fresh parsley
dumplings (below)

≈ In a medium, heavy saucepan, make a red-brown roux of lard and flour (page 15). Remove from the heat and stir in the vegetables. Return to the heat and cook until the vegetables are limp, about 5 minutes.

≈ In a deep skillet or large saucepan, bring the chicken stock to a boil. Add the roux and vegetables, 1 large spoonful at a time, whisking after each addition. Add the chicken and seasonings and simmer 30 minutes, uncovered.

≈ Meanwhile, prepare the dumplings.

DUMPLINGS

1¼ cups all-purpose flour
1½ tsp. baking powder
½ tsp. salt
1 tsp. dry mustard
¼ tsp. cayenne
2 eggs, lightly beaten
¼ cup milk
4 tbsp. butter, melted
¼ cup finely minced green onion
2 tbsp. chopped fresh parsley

≈ Mix the flour, baking powder and seasonings in 1 bowl. Combine the eggs, milk and butter in a second bowl. Pour the liquids into the dry ingredients and stir just until blended. Stir in the green onions and parsley.

≈ Drop spoonfuls of dough into the top of a steamer over simmering water. Cover and steam until the dumplings have risen slightly, about 7 minutes.

≈ Transfer the dumplings to the top of the stew and cook an additional 5 minutes, uncovered.

RABBIT STEW WITH LEEKS AND WILD MUSHROOMS

Wild mushrooms give this stew a heavenly accent. It is not a difficult dish. Start a day ahead by marinating the rabbit pieces, then use the marinade as part of the stewing liquid. The stew forms an excellent gravy.

SERVES 4

3½ lbs. rabbit, cut into 8 serving pieces
¼ cup olive oil
½ cup dry white wine
2 sprigs fresh tarragon, bruised to release flavor
1 bay leaf
2 cloves garlic, minced
2 carrots, peeled and sliced
1 leek, white part only, thinly sliced
dash of fresh-ground black pepper
½-1 cup all-purpose flour
2 tbsp. olive oil
1 leek, white part only, thinly sliced
1 cup dry white wine
2 cups poultry stock (page 16)
3 tbsp. butter
½ lb. wild mushrooms, any combination, quartered
4 cups hot noodles or cooked rice to serve

≈ In a glass or other non-reactive dish, make the marinade. Combine the olive oil, wine, tarragon, bay leaf, garlic, carrots, 1 leek and ground pepper. Marinate the rabbit for 24 hours in the refrigerator, turning and basting several times.

≈ Remove the rabbit and vegetables from marinade, and discard the bay leaf. Save the marinade. Mince the tarragon. Pat the rabbit pieces dry and dredge in flour.

≈ In a Dutch oven or large pot, heat 2 tablespoons olive oil. Brown the rabbit pieces on all sides, then remove. Saute the vegetables from the marinade, along with 1 fresh chopped leek. Add the tarragon, rabbit pieces, wine and stock to the pot and bring to a boil. Reduce the heat and simmer for 30 minutes, uncovered. Skim fat from surface.

≈ In a small skillet, melt the butter. Saute the mushrooms about 7 minutes. Add the mushrooms to the stew, and continue cooking until the rabbit is tender, about 30 minutes longer. Serve the stew over hot noodles or rice.

ROAST PORK WITH APPLE-WALNUT STUFFING

As elegant as it looks, this stuffed roast is not difficult to make. The most important tools are string to retie the roast after stuffing, a meat thermometer to determine when it is cooked through and a sharp carving knife. The stuffing is delicious – tart apples complemented by sauteed onions, the sweetness of golden raisins, the crunch of walnuts, and just a touch of cloves for spiciness. You may want to make some extra stuffing to serve on the side. The walnut halves should be cut into 2-4 pieces each, but not chopped any smaller. If the raisins are dry, soak in hot water for 20 minutes, then drain. You may substitute black raisins, if necessary, but the sweetness is not the same.

The roast is easiest to handle if you buy it butterflied and still in one piece. But if the roast is cut in half, you can still stuff it and tie it back together, it's just a little messier.

SERVES 8

6 tbsp. butter, divided
2 large Pippin or other tart apples, peeled, cored and cut into ½-in. chunks
½ cup chopped onion
2 ribs celery, chopped
1 clove garlic, minced
3 cups soft bread crumbs
1 cup walnut pieces
½ cup golden raisins
½ tsp. salt
¼ tsp. ground cloves
½ tsp. dry mustard
1 boned pork loin roast, 3-3½ lbs.
2-3 tbsp. vegetable oil

OVEN TEMPERATURE: 375°

≈ In a medium skillet, melt 3 tablespoons butter. Saute the apples until barely tender, 7-10 minutes. Remove the apples, set aside.

≈ Add 3 tablespoons butter to the skillet, and saute the onions, celery and garlic until onions are limp, about 5 minutes. Set aside.

≈ In large bowl, combine the apples, sauteed vegetables, bread crumbs, walnuts, raisins, salt, cloves and dry mustard. This stuffing is not intended to adhere in a solid mass, but it should be moist. If the pan juices are not sufficient, add a little milk. Set the stuffing aside.

≈ If the pork has not already been butterflied, cut it almost in half along its length. Spread it out and make lengthwise slashes along its thickest parts. If it is already cut in half, make 1 or 2 lengthwise slashes in each half.

≈ In a large skillet, heat the oil. Briefly cook the pork until the outside is browned, then remove from the pan. Set on a flat surface and spread it out with 4-6 lengths of kitchen string underneath. Mound the stuffing into the slashes. Carefully bring up the sides of the roast and tightly tie into a roll. If the stuffing falls out while you are reshaping the roast, just stuff it back in.

≈ Place the retied roast on a rack in a roasting pan. Cook at 375° until a thermometer inserted in the thickest part of the meat (but not inserted so far that it is measuring the temperature of the stuffing rather than the meat) registers at least 150°. This reading gives a very moist and slightly pink pork, and is hot enough to kill any trichinosis parasites. You may cook to 165° if you prefer well-done pork. To estimate cooking time, figure 25-30 minutes per pound, but rely on the thermometer to tell you when it is done.

≈ Remove the roast from the oven and let it sit for 15 minutes before carving.

NOTE:

≈ If there is any leftover stuffing, or if you have made extra, put it in a lightly buttered casserole dish and cook for 15-25 minutes (depending on quantity) at 375°.

PASTA AND RICE
MAIN DISHES

— ★ —

DUCK RICE

Use leftover duck meat for this delicious, one-dish meal. If you have only a few scraps of duck left, add them to the rice and use it as a side dish instead of a main dish.

SERVES 4-6

2 tbsp. duck fat or vegetable oil	
½ cup chopped onions	
1 cup sliced mushrooms	
1½ cups uncooked rice	
3 cups duck stock	
2 tsp. salt	
2 tsp. fresh thyme or ½ tsp. dried	
2 tsp. paprika	
½ tsp. black pepper	
2 tbsp. finely chopped celery leaves	
½ cup chopped green onions	
2 cups cooked duck meat, cut into strips or bite-size pieces	

OVEN TEMPERATURE: 350°

≈ In a skillet over medium heat, heat the duck fat or oil. Saute the onions and mushrooms until the onions are translucent, about 5 minutes. Add the rice and cook until it is lightly browned, about 5 minutes.

≈ Meanwhile, in a saucepan, bring the duck stock, seasonings and celery leaves to a boil. Combine the rice and stock mixtures in a lightly greased 2-quart casserole dish and stir in the duck and green onions. Cover and bake at 350° until all the liquids are absorbed and rice is cooked, about 1 hour.

DIRTY RICE

Dirty rice is a traditional Cajun dish served as an inexpensive main course or in smaller portions as a side dish. The taste of liver in dirty rice is subtle, and the gizzards give the dish an unexpectedly delicious, meaty taste. You may substitute the gizzard cooking water for part of the chicken stock, if it is rich. This recipe is baseline spicy – the Cajuns eat it hotter – so taste before serving and adjust seasonings accordingly.

SERVES 6 AS A SIDE DISH

½ lb. chicken gizzards, or a combination of hearts and gizzards
2 tbsp. vegetable oil
1 onion, chopped
1 rib celery, chopped
½ cup chopped green pepper
3 cloves garlic, minced
2 oz. chicken livers, trimmed and chopped
¼ lb. ground pork (not sausage)
1 cup chicken stock or canned broth
¼ tsp. black pepper
¼ tsp. salt
¼ tsp. cayenne
½ tsp. dry mustard
½ tsp. ground cumin
2 cups cooked white rice
2 green onions, chopped
2 tbsp. chopped fresh parsley

≈ Put the gizzards in a small saucepan, cover with water, and bring to a boil. Reduce the heat and simmer, uncovered, for 1 hour, adding extra water if necessary. Drain the gizzards and set aside until cool enough to chop.

≈ In a large saucepan over medium heat, heat the oil. Saute the onions, celery, green pepper and garlic until the vegetables are limp, about 5 minutes. Add the livers and pork and cook, stirring, until meat is browned. Add the chopped gizzards, along with chicken stock and spices and continue cooking until the liquids are slightly reduced. Taste and adjust seasonings.

≈ If the rice was not cooked with salt, you will need to add more salt here. Add the rice, green onions and parsley, and cook just until heated through, about 2 minutes.

RED BEANS AND RICE WITH TASSO AND ANDOUILLE

The use of two highly spiced meats means this is a very spicy dish. You can substitute ham hocks for the Tasso, but increase the amount of cayenne and black pepper or the end result will be very mild. The addition of vegetables at the end adds crunch to the texture.

MAKES 6-8 MAIN COURSE SERVINGS

2 cups (1 lb.) dried kidney beans, picked over
2-4 tbsp. vegetable oil or bacon drippings
2 cups chopped onion
1½ cups chopped celery
1½ cups chopped green pepper
2 cloves garlic, minced
8 oz. Tasso, cubed
8 oz. Andouille sausage, sliced
2 bay leaves
2 tsp. salt
2 tsp. ground cumin
1 tsp. dry mustard
1 tbsp. chopped fresh oregano or 1 tsp. dried
¼ tsp. black pepper
¼ tsp. cayenne
1 cup chopped green onion
½ cup chopped celery
½ cup chopped green pepper
¼ cup chopped fresh parsley
5-6 cups cooked rice to serve

≈ In 5 quarts water, soak the beans at least 4 hours or overnight. Drain, rinse and return to the large pot with 6 cups water. Bring to a boil, then reduce the heat and simmer, skimming the foam, while you prepare the vegetables.

≈ In the meanwhile, in a skillet, heat the oil or drippings and saute the 2 cups onion, 1½ cups celery, 1½ cups green pepper and 2 cloves garlic until wilted, about 5 minutes. Unless you use a very large skillet, it is easier to saute the vegetables in 2 batches. Add the vegetables to the beans, along with the Tasso, sausage and seasonings and continue simmering, stirring occasionally, until beans are tender, 1-1½ hours. Add extra water if necessary. Taste and adjust seasonings.

≈ Just before serving, stir in the remaining green onions, celery, green pepper and parsley and mix well. Serve over rice.

RED BEANS AND RICE WITH TASSO AND ANDOUILLE

MEATLESS RED BEANS AND RICE

MEATLESS RED BEANS AND RICE

Serve this flavorful, slow-cooked dish with salsa and sour cream. Extra vegetables are added near the end for crunch.

SERVES 6-8

2 cups (1 lb.) dry kidney beans, picked over
3 tbsp. olive oil
1 large onion, chopped
4 garlic cloves, minced
2 ribs celery, chopped
1 carrot, chopped
1 green pepper, seeded and chopped
1 tbsp. salt
¼ tsp. cayenne
¼ tsp. white pepper
¼ tsp. black pepper
1 tsp. dried thyme
1½ tsp. ground cumin
1 tsp. dry mustard
1 bay leaf
6-oz. can tomato paste
½ cup dry red wine
few drops of Tabasco sauce
1 rib celery, chopped
½ cup chopped green pepper
4 green onions, chopped
4-5 cups cooked rice to serve
sour cream

SALSA

2 large tomatoes, seeded and chopped
4 green onions, chopped
½ long mild chile, such as Anaheim or poblano
1 tbsp. fresh chopped parsley
1 tbsp. white wine vinegar
1 tbsp. olive oil
few drops Tabasco, to taste

≈ In 5 quarts water, soak the beans at least 4 hours or overnight. Drain, rinse and return to the large pot with 6 cups water. Bring to a boil, then reduce the heat and simmer, skimming the foam, while you prepare the vegetables.

≈ In the meanwhile, in a skillet, heat the oil and saute the onion, garlic, celery, carrot and green pepper until wilted, about 5 minutes. Add the vegetables to the beans, along with the seasonings, tomato paste and wine and continue simmering, stirring occasionally.

≈ After about 30 minutes, taste the sauce, then add Tabasco to taste, and adjust the other seasonings. Cook the beans until tender, a total of 1-1½ hours.

≈ Meanwhile, in a bowl, combine all the salsa ingredients. Allow the flavors to blend for about 1 hour, then taste and add more Tabasco sauce if desired.

≈ Just before serving, stir the chopped celery, green pepper and green onions in to the bean mixture. Serve the beans over the rice, then top with salsa and sour cream.

DUCK WITH SHRIMP AND FETTUCINE

Fresh herbs and shrimp complement the duck flavour in this meaty sauce.

SERVES 6-8

2 tbsp. olive oil
4 garlic cloves, minced
½ cup chopped onion
½ cup chopped green pepper
4 tomatoes, seeded and diced
2 cups sliced mushrooms
8-oz. can tomato sauce
1 tbsp. fresh-squeezed lemon juice
2 tbsp. chopped fresh basil
1½ tsp. chopped fresh rosemary
1 tsp. paprika
¼ tsp. black pepper
1 tsp. salt
¼ tsp. cayenne
1½ cups duck or chicken stock
1-1½ lbs. dry fettucine
2 cups cooked duck meat, cut into strips or bite-size pieces
½ lb. medium shrimp, shelled and deveined
1 cup chopped green onions
2 tbsp. chopped fresh parsley
Parmesan cheese

≈ In a large saucepan or stockpot over medium heat, heat the oil. Saute the garlic, onion and green pepper until limp, 5 minutes. Add the tomatoes, mushrooms, tomato sauce, lemon juice, seasonings and stock and simmer, 10 minutes.

≈ While the sauce is simmering, cook the fettucine in a large pot of boiling water. Drain and toss with a little olive oil to keep it from sticking.

≈ Add the duck to the sauce and simmer 5 minutes, uncovered. Add the shrimp and cook until they are opaque and tightly curled, 2–3 minutes. Stir in the green onions and parsley and serve over the fettucine, topped with Parmesan cheese.

FETTUCINE WITH VEAL AND ARTICHOKES

Use fresh artichokes for the fullest flavor, and fresh herbs because the sauce does not cook long enough to soften dried herbs. The result is a creamy, slightly spicy sauce.

SERVES 4

¾ lb. boneless veal, cut into 2- × ½-inch strips
1 tsp. salt
⅛ tsp. white pepper
⅛ tsp. cayenne
⅛ tsp. black pepper
¼ tsp. dry mustard
3 tbsp. all-purpose flour
3 tbsp. olive oil
2 cloves garlic, minced
1½ cups sliced fresh mushrooms
4 green onions, chopped
1 tbsp. chopped fresh basil
1 tbsp. chopped fresh oregano
2 tsp. fresh thyme
1½ cups light cream or half-and-half
¼ tsp. salt
2 artichoke hearts, cooked and sliced
2 green onions, chopped
½–¾ lb. dry fettucine or other pasta, cooked

≈ In a small bowl, combine salt, peppers, mustard and 2 tbsp. flour. Toss the veal with the seasoning mix until all the veal is coated and all the seasoning is absorbed.

≈ In a skillet over medium heat, heat the olive oil. Saute the veal until it is browned, 6–8 minutes. Remove the meat from the skillet and set aside.

≈ If needed, add another 1–2 tbsp. olive oil to the skillet. Saute the garlic, mushrooms, 4 green onions, and fresh herbs until limp, about 5 minutes.

≈ In a small bowl or measuring cup, mix 1 tbps. flour with 2 tbsp. cream until smooth, then stir in the remaining cream. Add the cream, salt and veal to the skillet and stir well. Heat the sauce until it barely starts to bubble, then taste, and adjust the seasonings. Add the sliced artichoke hearts and the remaining green onions and cook just enough to heat through. Serve over the pasta.

CRAWFISH AND TASSO IN CREAM SAUCE OVER FETTUCINE

This quick-and-easy dish makes a rich, creamy, yet spicy sauce. It's also good made with large shrimp instead of crawfish tails.

SERVES 4-6

6 tbsp. butter
1 cup chopped green onions
3 cloves garlic, minced
½ cup dry white wine
½ cup dry white wine
½ cup seafood stock (page 17) or clam juice, divided
¾ cup diced Tasso
¼ cup all-purpose flour
2 cups cooked and shelled crawfish tails
2 cups half-and-half
salt to taste
hot cooked fettucine to serve

≈ In a large skillet, melt the butter. Saute the green onions and garlic about 2 minutes. Add wine, ¼ cup seafood stock and the Tasso and cook until bubbly. Reduce the heat and simmer until liquid is reduced slightly, about 10 minutes.

≈ Dissolve the flour in remaining ¼ cup seafood stock, then add to the sauce and stir until smooth. Stir in the crawfish tails and the half-and-half. Mix well and heat just until bubbly. Taste and adjust salt. Serve over fettucine.

ABOVE *A lone cypress tree rises from Lake Palourde against the setting sun.*

RIGHT *New Orleans has never needed an excuse for a parade or a celebration, but Mardi Gras is its biggest — a long, noisy and wild festival that brings people from all over the world to celebrate Fat Tuesday, the last day before Lent.*

PASTA

ITALIANS WERE AMONG THE ETHNIC GROUPS TO MIGRATE TO *Louisiana during the 19th century, many of them from Sicily. Like every other group of settlers or traders, the Italians in-fluenced the cuisine of Louisiana. here are four distinctive dishes that combine pasta with crawfish, Andouille sausage and other prominent ingredients of Louisiana cooking.*

≈ *The recipes call for fettucine, but you can use almost any pasta, although some type of flat noodle is recommended. The measurements are for dry fettucine, but fresh pasta is even more delicious. Just remember that fresh pasta weighs more (roughly 50 percent more, although that figure varies widely) and you will need to increase the weight specified for dry pasta to arrive at the same cooked quantity. And it's fun to experiment with the different flavors of pasta that are available at gourmet stores.*

≈ *For 1 pound of pasta, bring 2 quarts of water to a boil. Add 1 tbsp. olive oil, 1 tbsp. salt and 1 crushed clove of garlic, then add the pasta. Boil, uncovered, tasting frequently until it is cooked to your taste.*

≈ *Drain the pasta in a collander, but don't rinse it. Toss it with a little olive oil to keep it from sticking. The pasta may be kept warm over simmering water.*

FETTUCINE WITH SHRIMP AND ANDOUILLE SAUSAGE

This is a moderately spicy dish, with the pepper flavor largely provided by the sausage, so be sure to taste and adjust the seasonings. This recipe uses a combination of fresh tomatoes and canned tomato sauce for speed, but you can substitute more fresh tomatoes for the sauce if you have the extra time to cook it down.

SERVES 4

2 tbsp. olive oil
2 tomatoes, seeded and chopped
1 cup chopped onion
1 rib celery, chopped
¼ cup chopped green pepper
1 tbsp. chopped fresh jalapeño
2 cloves garlic, minced
8-oz. can tomato sauce
½ cup seafood stock (page 17)
¾ tsp. salt
¼ tsp. black pepper
1 tbsp. chopped fresh basil
½ lb. andouille sausage, sliced
cayenne (optional)
½ lb. medium shrimp, shelled and deveined
½-¾ lb. dry fettucine or other pasta

≈ In a large saucepan or deep skillet, heat the olive oil. Saute the tomatoes, onion, celery, green pepper, jalapeño and garlic until the vegetables are limp, about 5 minutes. Add the tomato sauce, seafood stock, salt, pepper, basil and sausage and cook until tomato is cooked down and liquids are reduced, forming a thick, rich broth, 10-15 minutes. Tase and adjust seasonings. If you want it spicier, this is the time to add cayenne in ⅛ teaspoon increments.

≈ While the sauce is simmering, cook the fettucine in a large pot of boiling water. Drain and toss with a little olive oil to keep it from sticking.

≈ Add the shrimp to the sauce and cook just until they are opaque and tightly curled, 2-3 minutes. Serve the sauce over the fettucine.

VEGETABLES

— ★ —

CORN MAQUE CHOUX

There are many variations of this spicy corn dish, which can be made on the stovetop or in the oven. It's best made with fresh corn cut off the cob in your kitchen, but if you can't find fresh corn on the cob, use frozen corn kernels.

SERVES 3-4

1 tbsp. butter
2 tbsp. vegetable oil
2 cups corn kernels (4–6 fresh ears)
½ onion, chopped
1 garlic clove, minced
¼ cup chopped green onion
1 tbsp. sugar
¼ tsp. black pepper
½ tsp. salt
¼ tsp. cayenne
½ cup poultry stock (page 16) or canned chicken broth
1 tbsp. butter
1 egg, lightly beaten
½ cup milk

≈ In a skillet over medium heat, melt 1 tablespoon butter with the oil. Saute the corn, onion, garlic and green pepper, stirring often, until the onion is limp and transparent, about 5 minutes. Add the seasonings, and stir until combined. Add the stock and reduce heat to very low and simmer until liquid has almost evaporated, stirring often. Stir in 1 tablespoon butter until melted and mixed in.

≈ In a small bowl, mix together the egg and milk, whisking until frothy. Add to the corn, stirring well, until the mixture is heated through.

SHRIMP-STUFFED ARTICHOKES

Tiny shrimp and Gruyère cheese make a delicious hot filling for artichokes. Serve these as a first course, or pour the filling over the top of toasted English muffins.

SERVES 6 AS AN APPETIZER OR 3 FOR A LUNCHEON

2 tbsp. butter
1 cup sliced mushrooms
1 clove garlic, minced
3 tbsp. all-purpose flour
1 cup seafood stock (page 17) or clam juice, divided
1/4 cup dry white wine
dash of salt
dash of black pepper
dash of cayenne
2 tbsp. chopped fresh basil or 1/2 tsp. dried
1/2 lb. bay shrimp, cooked and cleaned
1/3 cup grated Gruyère cheese
1/3 cup chopped green onions
6 artichoke hearts, cooked and trimmed
6 tbsp. grated Gruyère cheese

OVEN TEMPERATURE: 350°

≈ In a medium skillet, melt the butter. Saute the mushrooms and garlic 7–8 minutes.

≈ Dissolve the flour in 1/4 cup stock. Stir in the remaining stock, then stir into the mushrooms. Add the wine and seasonings, and cook until the mixture is thick and bubbly. Stir in the shrimp, cheese and green onions, and cook over a low heat just until cheese is melted, about 2–3 minutes.

≈ Divide the shrimp filling among the artichoke hearts. Top each with 1 tablespoon cheese. Place in baking dish and bake at 350° until cheese topping is melted, about 10 minutes. Serve hot.

VARIATIONS:

≈ If you start with whole artichokes, add the tender part of the stem and leaf scrapings from 3 artichokes to the filling when you add the shrimp. You may also stuff 4 whole cooked artichokes, with the chokes removed, and serve a dipping sauce on the side for the leaves.

RIGHT The explorer Jean Baptiste Le Moyne, Sieur de Bienville, saw in the swamps of Louisiana the vision of another Paris. He founded the city of New Orleans in 1718, with this riverfront square at the center. Today Jackson Square is at the heart of the thriving Vieux Carré, or French Quarter.

DINNER FOR THE THIN (OR WOULD-BE THIN)

★

Shrimp Salsa with crackers and crudites
PAGE 28

★

Tomato-Basil Salad
PAGE 33

★

Grilled Shark
PAGES 60–61

★

Grilled Spicy Vegetables and Potatoes
PAGE 89

★

Fresh fruit

GRILLED SPICY VEGETABLES AND POTATOES

Cooked with a minimum of fat, these grilled vegetables are an easy side dish when you're barbecuing meat or fish. Just arrange them around the edges of the grill.

sliced vegetables
olive oil
paprika and cumin or other spices
salt

≈ Slice red potatoes, zucchini or eggplant about ¼ inch thick or slightly thicker. Zucchini and eggplant are attractive cut at a diagonal; cut crooked-neck squash in half lengthwise.

≈ Brush the cut edges lightly with olive oil and sprinkle with your favorite spices – paprika and cumin work well in this recipe, dried herbs do not. Lightly salt the potatoes, if desired.

≈ When the barbecue coals are no longer flaming, place the vegetables on the grill. Turn once during cooking: squash cooks quickly, about 5 minutes; eggplant takes 1-2 minutes longer; potatoes take about 10 minutes. The cooking times are a little shorter if the vegetables are directly over the coals instead of around the edges.

GREENS AND TASSO

GREENS AND TASSO

Greens cooked with pork are a long-time staple of Southern cuisine. Here I use Tasso to give it a Louisiana twist. You can use chard, collards, kale, mustard or turnip greens, or a combination. Just remember that a huge pile of crisp greens will cook down to a very small mound.

SERVES 4

2 bunches greens
½ onion, chopped
3 oz. Tasso, chopped

≈ Wash the greens very thoroughly, until all the sand is removed. This may take 3 or 4 washings. Tear the greens into pieces and chop the stems.

≈ Put the greens into a pot with the onion, Tasso and 1 cup water. Bring to a boil, then cover and reduce the heat and simmer, stirring occasionally, until stems are tender, about 40 minutes. Drain off any excess water, and serve.

PEPPERED POTATOES

Broiled or grilled, these potato slices make a tasty side dish without the mess or large amounts of oil needed for French fries. They are very peppery, so beware!

SERVES 4

1 lb. red potatoes, unpeeled, cut into ¼-in. slices
olive oil
2 tsp. salt
1 tsp. white pepper
½ tsp. black pepper
½ tsp. cayenne

≈ Brush both sides of the potato slices with a scant amount of olive oil. Combine the spices in a small bowl, then sprinkle on top of the sliced potatoes.

≈ Put the potato slices under broiler or on top of a barbecue grill and cook for 3-4 minutes. Turn over and cook another 3-4 minutes.

SPICY GREEN BEANS

Marinate these beans early in the day, and you'll have a spicy dish by dinner. These make an easy and convenient addition to a picnic or tailgate party.

SERVES 3-4

1 lb. fresh green beans, topped and tailed
2 tbsp. vegetable oil
2 tbsp. white wine vinegar
1 tbsp. fresh-squeezed lemon juice
1 tsp. Creole mustard
1 garlic clove, minced
1 green onion, minced
1 tsp. red-pepper flakes
¼ tsp. salt

≈ Cook the green beans in boiling water until just tender, 3-4 minutes. Drain and plunge into cold water, then drain well again.

≈ In glass or other non-reactive dish whisk together all the remaining ingredients. Add the beans and stir to coat thoroughly. Refrigerate at least 3 hours. Serve cold.

DEEP-FRIED EGGPLANT

Serve this spicy, crispy eggplant as an appetizer for those informal dinners when your guests are clustered in the kitchen, or as a side dish.

SERVES 5-6

½ cup grated Parmesan cheese
½ cup cornmeal
1 tsp. cayenne
1 tsp. onion powder
1 tsp. celery salt
½ tsp. salt
½ tsp. garlic powder
2 eggs, lightly beaten
½ cup milk
few drops of Tabasco sauce
1 large eggplant, cut into ¼-in. thick slices
vegetable oil for frying

≈ In a bowl, combine the cheese, cornmeal and spices. In a second bowl, combine the eggs, milk and Tabasco sauce.

≈ Dip the eggplant slices into the cornmeal mixture, then into egg mixture, then into the cornmeal a second time.

≈ In a deep skillet or wok, heat 2–3 inches of oil to 350°. With tongs, gently drop 3–5 slices of eggplant into the oil, taking care not to crowd, and fry until golden brown on both sides, turning once, about 2 minutes a side. Drain briefly on paper towels and keep warm in the oven while you fry the remaining eggplant slices. Make sure the oil returns to 350° before frying the next batch.

SCALLOPED POTATOES WITH TASSO

This is a Louisiana variation on a classic French dish, with Tasso ham and green onions adding a Cajun flavor. You can use another type of ham, but you'll need to add extra seasoning that the Tasso provides here. This dish can be prepared in advance and refrigerated, with the seasoned cream poured over it just before it goes in the oven.

SERVES 6-8

2½–3 lbs. red potatoes
2 tbsp. butter or vegetable oil
1 onion, thinly sliced
¾ cup diced Tasso
1 cup chopped green onion
1 cup grated cheddar cheese
1 cup grated Gruyère cheese
1-1½ cups heavy cream
1 tsp. paprika
1 tsp. dry mustard
½ tsp. salt
¼ tsp. black pepper

OVEN TEMPERATURE: 425°

≈ Leaving the skin on the potatoes, slice them thinly and place in a bowl of cold water.

≈ In a small skillet, heat the butter or oil. Saute the onion until lightly browned, 8-10 minutes.

≈ Drain the water off the potatoes and pat them dry with paper towels.

≈ In a large, ungreased casserole or baking pan (at least 9 × 9 inches), put a single layer of potatoes. Follow with some of the sauteed onion, Tasso, green onion and the cheeses. Continue layering until you've used up the ingredients, ending with the cheese.

≈ In a small saucepan, mix the cream with the seasonings and heat until just shy of a boil. Pour over the potatoes to a depth of ¼-½ inch. Bake, uncovered, at 425°, basting with pan liquids once or twice, until potatoes are tender and most of the cream is absorbed, about 45 minutes.

SIDE DISHES

—★—

HUSHPUPPIES

Hushpuppies are traditionally paired with Fried Catfish (page 59), but they are a great side dish with any number of entrees, from Grilled Shark (pages 60–61) to fried chicken. You can use the same oil to fry hushpuppies and fish, but cook the hushpuppies first, then keep them warm in the oven.

MAKES ABOUT 20

1 cup cornmeal
½ cup corn flour
1 tbsp. baking powder
½ tsp. salt
½ tsp. garlic powder
¼ tsp. cayenne
1 egg, lightly beaten
1 cup milk
2 tbsp. butter
¼ cup finely chopped green onion
vegetable oil for frying

≈ Combine the dry ingredients, then stir in the egg.

≈ In a medium saucepan, bring the milk and butter to a boil. Stir in the cornmeal mixture until smooth, then add the green onions. Remove from the heat and let sit until it is cool enough to handle. Roll the mixture into balls the size of large walnuts or small plums.

≈ In a deep skillet or wok, heat the 3–4 inches of oil to 350°. Drop the dough balls into the oil a few at a time, taking care not to crowd, and fry until golden brown, turning once, about 3 minutes a side. Remove from oil and keep warm in the oven while you fry the remaining hush-puppies. Make sure the oil returns to 350° before frying the next batch.

CORNBREAD

This is a dense, moist cornbread, perfect for stuffings, such as for Crawfish Bisque (pages 43–46). It's also a good, basic cornbread to which you can add extras like grated cheese, chili and corn kernels.

MAKES 9 SQUARES

⅓ cup all-purpose flour
1 cup cornmeal
¾ tsp. salt
1 tsp. sugar
1 tbsp. baking powder
2 eggs, lightly beaten
1 cup milk
¼ cup butter, melted

OVEN TEMPERATURE: 400°

≈ Lightly butter an 8-inch square baking pan, or spray with non-stick spray.

≈ In a medium bowl, combine all the dry ingredients. In a small bowl, mix together the eggs, milk and butter. Pour these into the flour mixture and stir by hand, making sure there are no lumps.

≈ Pour into the baking pan and bake at 400° until a knife inserted into the cornbread comes out clean, 18-22 minutes. Cut into 9 squares, like a tic-tac-toe game.

OYSTER STUFFING

I like to buy extra chicken hearts and gizzards to give this stuffing extra flavor. Use this to stuff a bird, or cook it as a stand-alone side dish.

SERVES 6–8 AS A SIDE DISH

heart and gizzard from bird to be stuffed, plus several extras if possible
6 tbsp. butter
1½ cups chopped onion
1 cup chopped celery
4 tbsp. chopped fresh parsley
1 tbsp. chopped fresh tarragon, or 1 tsp. dried
1 tsp. salt
½ tsp. black pepper
7 cups stale bread cubes (preferably French, Italian or sourdough)
1 pint oysters, shucked, drained and cut into bite-size pieces
1 egg, lightly beaten

OVEN TEMPERATURE: 350°

≈ In a saucepan, simmer the giblets in water to cover for 1 hour. Set aside and reserve the cooking water in case it is needed for moistening bread.

≈ In a skillet over medium heat, melt the butter. Saute the vegetables until limp, about 5 minutes. Add herbs, salt and pepper and remove from the heat. Chop the giblets and mix them in with the vegetables.

≈ Put the bread cubes in a greased 2-quart casserole dish. Add the vegetable-giblet mixture, oysters and the egg: the bread should be well-moistened but not mushy. If the egg and juices from the vegetables and the oysters do not moisten bread sufficiently, add the oyster liquor, or giblet cooking water, or milk.

≈ Bake, covered, at 350° for 25 minutes, then bake an additional 5 minutes, uncovered.

BAKED CRAWFISH-CORNBREAD STUFFING

The tastes and textures of crawfish tails, sauteed mushrooms and toasted pecans set each other off nicely in this dish. Use it as a side dish with roast duck or poultry.

SERVES 6-8

1 cup pecan halves
2 tbsp. butter
1 cup chopped onion
1 cup chopped celery
½ cup chopped green pepper
2 cups sliced mushrooms
2 tbsp. chopped fresh parsley
½ cup shelled crawfish tail meat, each cut into 2 or 3 pieces
1 tsp. salt
1 tsp. dried thyme
½ tsp. white pepper
½ tsp. dry mustard
¼ tsp. cayenne
¼ tsp. black pepper
3 cups crumbled cornbread (pages 96–97)
1-1½ cups seafood stock (page 17) or clam juice

OVEN TEMPERATURE: 350°

≈ Toast the pecans by spreading them in a single layer on cookie sheet. Bake at 350° until they appear slightly darker and drier, 10–15 minutes. Set aside to cool.

≈ In a medium skillet, melt the butter. Saute the vegetables and parsley until the vegetables are limp, about 5 minutes. Stir in the crawfish tails, pecans and the seasonings.

≈ Lightly butter or oil a 2-quart casserole dish. Mix together the cornbread crumbs, the vegetable-crawfish mixture and enough seafood stock so the mixture is thoroughly moistened but not mushy. Spoon into the casserole and smooth the top. Bake at 350° for 20 minutes.

TASSO BISCUITS

Serve this Cajun version of buttermilk biscuits piping hot with butter. Or, spread with mustard and add ham for tiny sandwiches.

MAKES 16–20 BISCUITS

2 cups all-purpose flour
1 tbsp. baking powder
1 tsp. dry mustard
½ tsp. baking soda
2 tsp. sugar
½ tsp. salt
⅓ cup minced or ground Tasso
3 tbsp. finely chopped green onions
3 tbsp. butter
3 tbsp. lard
⅔ cup buttermilk
heavy cream

OVEN TEMPERATURE: 400°

≈ In a large bowl, combine all the dry ingredients with the ham and onions. Using a pair of sharp knives or a pastry cutter, cut in the butter and lard until the flour is the consistency of cornmeal. Mix in the buttermilk.

≈ Roll out the dough to ½-inch thick and cut into 2-inch circles. Put on an ungreased cooking sheet and brush tops with cream. Bake at 400° until the biscuits are risen and tops are just slightly browned, about 20 minutes.

TRINITY RICE WITH ALMONDS

Made with onions, peppers and celery – the Holy Trinity of Cajun cooking – this Louisiana version of rice pilaf has the added bonus of almonds.

MAKES 8 SIDE-DISH SERVINGS

2 tbsp. butter or olive oil
½ cup chopped celery
½ cup chopped green pepper
½ cup chopped onion
2 cloves garlic, minced
½ cup blanched almonds, slivered or sliced
1 tsp. Worcestershire sauce
1½ tsp. salt
¼ tsp. black pepper
1 tomato, seeded and chopped
½ cup chopped green onion
2 tbsp. chopped fresh parsley
2 cups white rice

≈ In a medium skillet, heat the butter or olive oil. Saute the celery, green pepper, onion and garlic until limp, about 5 minutes. Remove the vegetables and set aside. If there is no oil left in pan, add about 1 tablespoon more. Add the almonds, and stir frequently until they are lightly browned. Add the Worcestershire and stir well. Set aside.

≈ In a large saucepan, bring 3½ cups water to a boil. Add the salt, pepper, tomato, green onion, parsley, sauteed vegetables and almonds and return to a boil. Add the rice, stir well and reduce the heat to very low, cover and cook until all the water is absorbed and rice is fluffy, 20-25 minutes. Or, to avoid scorching, you may turn off the burner and let rice cook in its own steam heat for the last few minutes.

SWEETS AND DESSERTS

———— ★ ————

BANANAS FOSTER

Quick and easy, this is a classic New Orleans dessert with a Caribbean flavor. If you double the recipe, use a large skillet so you can flambe all the bananas at once; the liqueur does not flame as well the second time. For safety reasons, you'll need a long, fireplace-type match and a long-handled spoon.

SERVES 2

3 tbsp. butter
3 tbsp. brown sugar
1/2 tsp. cinnamon
2 bananas, peeled, cut in half, then sliced lengthwise
3 tbsp. brandy
3 tbsp. banana-flavored liqueur
vanilla ice cream to serve

≈ Spoon the ice cream into dishes ahead of time.

≈ In a skillet, melt the butter. Stir in the brown sugar and cinnamon, then add the bananas and saute about 1½ minutes. Add the liqueurs and allow the mixture to heat for a moment – too short and it won't flame, too long and the alcohol will evaporate. Flame with a long match. With a long-handled spoon, spoon the flaming syrup over the bananas until the flame goes out.

≈ Put the bananas on top of ice cream, and spoon some of the syrup over the top. Serve immediately.

PRALINES

PRALINES

These chewy, buttery pralines are a rich New Orleans treat. Unlike many candies, where the nuts are added at the end, the pecans are cooked in the hot sugar and butter mixture to infuse the candy with the taste of pecans. This candy does not keep well.

MAKES ABOUT 24

1 cup (2 sticks) butter
2 cups granulated sugar
1 cup brown sugar
½ cup heavy cream
1 cup milk
1 cup coarsely chopped pecans
2 cups pecan halves
2 tbsp. light corn syrup
2 tbsp. vanilla

≈ Lightly butter 2 large cookie sheets, or line them with buttered parchment or aluminum foil. You will need a candy thermometer.

≈ In a large, heavy saucepan over low heat, melt the butter. As soon as the butter is melted, without allowing it to brown, stir in the sugars and cream. When sugar is dissolved and mixture is smooth, add the milk and chopped pecans and continue cooking a few minutes, until mixture is smooth and heated through. Stir in the pecan halves, corn syrup and vanilla.

≈ Cook over medium heat, stirring constantly, until mixture reaches 238° on the candy thermometer.

≈ Working quickly, spoon the mixture onto the cookie sheets. The mixture will be runny, but will set into patties. When they have cooled, remove them from the cookie sheets and wrap individually in foil or plastic wrap. Store in an airtight container.

APPLE BREAD PUDDING

APPLE BREAD PUDDING

Using apples, this recipe is a variation on the traditional bread pudding with pecans and raisins, and is topped with a delicious hot cinnamon sauce.

SERVES 8

2 small, tart apples, peeled, cored and cut into 12-14 wedges
2 tbsp. butter
2 tbsp. brown sugar
½ tsp. cinnamon
½ cup milk
3 eggs
⅓ cup brown sugar
⅓ cup granulated sugar
1 tsp. vanilla
½ tsp. grated nutmeg
1 tsp. cinnamon
2 cups milk
7 cups dry bread cubes (French, Italian or sourdough)
sweetened whipped cream to serve

HOT CINNAMON SAUCE

¼ cup butter
1 cup brown sugar
1 tsp. cinnamon
1 cup half-and-half, warmed
2 tbsp. rum or 2 tsp. rum flavoring

OVEN TEMPERATURE: 300° AND 425°

≈ In a skillet over medium heat, melt the butter. Saute the apples, 5 minutes. Add 2 tablespoons brown sugar, ½ teaspoon cinnamon and ½ cup milk and simmer until the apples are barely tender, 10-15 minutes. Set aside.

≈ In a large bowl, beat the eggs until frothy, about 2 minutes. Beat in the sugars, taking care that the brown sugar has no lumps. Add the vanilla, nutmeg, remaining cinnamon and milk, and mix well. Add the bread cubes and apples and mix by hand. Let the bread sit until liquids are absorbed, stirring occasionally, about 45 minutes.

≈ Lightly grease a 9-inch square baking pan. Turn the bread into the pan and bake at 300° for 35 minutes, then increase temperature to 425° and bake an additional 10 minutes, until the top is slightly crusty.

≈ Meanwhile, prepare the sauce. In a small saucepan, heat the butter until just melted. Stir in the sugar and cinnamon until smooth. Whisk in the half-and-half and rum and heat until just shy of boiling.

≈ Cut the pudding into 8 pieces. Put some hot cinnamon sauce into 8 shallow bowls. Put a piece of bread pudding on top, and top pudding with sweetened whipped cream.

BASIC PIECRUST

This recipe makes an 8-inch crust. For some recipes, such as Sweet-Potato and Pecan Pie (page 105), you'll want to bake the crust blind about 5 minutes before adding the filling. This will keep the crust from getting soggy.

1 cup all-purpose flour
pinch of salt
3 tbsp. chilled butter
3 tbsp. chilled lard
1 tbsp. sugar
2-3 tbsp. ice water

OVEN TEMPERATURE: 400°

≈ In a bowl, mix together the flour, salt, butter and lard. Using a pastry cutter or a pair of sharp knives, cut in the shortening until the mixture has a coarse grain, with some bits of shortening the size of peas. Sprinkle the ice water over surface of the mixture, 1 tablespoon at a time, mixing with your hands until dough sticks together in a ball. You may also do this in a food processor, but use a very light touch or the dough will be tough. Mix in the last 1-2 tablespoons of water by hand so you can feel when it's ready.

≈ Wrap the dough in plastic wrap and refrigerate for at least 1 hour, then remove from refrigerator 1 hour before shaping. Chilling makes the dough easier to handle.

≈ Roll out the dough on a lightly floured board with a floured rolling pin, until it is about 10 inches in diameter. Fold in quarters, place in an 8-inch pie pan, and unfold. Trim the crust to a 1-inch overhang. Roll up the overhang and pinch into a fluted edge.

≈ Bake at 400°, about 5 minutes for a partially cooked crust, or until lightly browned, about 12 minutes, for a completely cooked crust.

CHOCOLATE-PECAN PIE

It won't take a big piece of this chocolaty pie to satisfy a sweet tooth. Serve it at room temperature, topped with sweetened whipped cream.

SERVES 6–8

4 oz. semisweet chocolate
4 tbsp. unsalted butter
1/3 cup heavy cream
1/2 cup light corn syrup
3 tbsp. bourbon
2 eggs, separated
1/2 cup sugar
1 1/2 cups pecan halves
8-inch piecrust (see Basic Piecrust recipe on this page)

OVEN TERMPERATURE: 350°

≈ In the top of a double boiler, over hot – not boiling – water, melt the chocolate, butter and cream, stirring until smooth. Set aside and let cool, about 10 minutes.

≈ While the chocolate is cooling, mix the corn syrup and bourbon with the egg yolks. Gradually add about one-third of the chocolate to the eggs yolks, then add the yolks to the remaining chocolate and set aside.

≈ Beat the egg whites until soft peaks form, adding the sugar a little at a time. Gently fold the egg whites into the chocolate mixture until no streaks of white remain. Stir in the pecans, and pour filling into pie shell.

≈ Bake the pie at 350° for 45–50 minutes. The filling will set, but will still leave a residue of chocolate on a knife. As it cools, cracks may form in the top. That is normal.

VARIATION:

≈ Omit the bourbon, and add 1 tbsp. powdered instant coffee to the chocolate while it is melting, and add 1 tsp. vanilla to the egg yolks.

SWEET-POTATO AND PECAN PIE

Two Louisiana favorites are combined in this rich pie: a smooth, spicy sweet-potato filling and a sweet crunchy pecan topping. Serve this pie topped with sweetened whipped cream.

MAKES 1 PIE

8- or 9-inch pie shell, partially baked (page 104)

FILLING

6 tbsp. brown sugar, packed
3 tbsp. granulated sugar
1½ tbsp. unsalted butter
1 egg, lightly beaten
1½ tbsp. heavy cream
1½ tbsp. vanilla
¼ tsp. salt
¾ tsp. cinnamon
¼ tsp. ground allspice
¼ tsp. grated nutmeg
¼ tsp. ground ginger
1½ cups sweet potato pulp (see Note below)

TOPPING

¼ cup brown sugar
¼ cup granulated sugar
¼ cup light corn syrup
1 egg
1 tbsp. unsalted butter, melted
1 tsp. vanilla
pinch of salt
1 cup pecan halves

OVEN TEMPERATURE: 325°

≈ To make the filling, in a bowl, cream the sugars and butter together. When mixture is smooth, add the egg, cream, vanilla and seasonings and mix until smooth. Add the sweet potato pulp and mix again until smooth.

≈ To make the topping, in a bowl, mix the sugars with the corn syrup until there are no lumps in the brown sugar. Beat in the egg, butter, vanilla and salt until the mixture is frothy, about 1 minute. Stir in the pecans.

≈ Pour the sweet-potato filling into the pie shell. Pour the pecan syrup over the top, spreading to make sure filling is completely covered. Bake at 325° until a knife inserted in center comes out clean, about 1¾ hours.

NOTE:

≈ You can use canned sweet potatoes, but make sure they aren't packed with syrup. Otherwise, bake your own sweet potatoes to make the pulp.

CHOCOLATE ESPRESSO CAKE

Serve this very rich and dense cake in small wedges. It cooks slowly, and will fall in the center after you remove it from the oven. If that bothers you, fill the center with whipped cream. Otherwise, use cream only as a garnish. Use only high-quality chocolate. The cake is best served at room temperature, so that the full flavor is not masked by the cold.

SERVES 12–16

1 lb. bittersweet chocolate
1 cup (2 sticks) unsalted butter
4 tsp. powdered espresso
1/2 cup sugar
5 eggs
sweetened whipped cream
chocolate-covered espresso beans

OVEN TEMPERATURE: 250°

≈ Butter the bottom and sides of an 8-inch springform pan.

≈ In the top of a double boiler, over hot (not boiling) water, melt the chocolate and butter.

≈ Dissolve the espresso powder in 2 tablespoons boiling water and add to the melting chocolate. Stir frequently, until the mixture is smooth. Add the sugar and continue to cook until sugar is dissolved, about 5 minutes. (Be sure the water is not boiling or it may give chocolate a slightly scorched flavor.) Remove from the heat and let cool 10 minutes.

≈ In a large bowl, beat the eggs until frothy. Add a small amount of chocolate to the eggs, a spoonful at a time, incorporating the chocolate slowly so it does not cook the eggs. Mix the eggs with the remaining chocolate and stir well. Pour into the buttered pan. Bake until a pick inserted in the center comes out clean, about 2 hours. Cool to room temperature.

≈ Just before serving, garnish with whipped cream and espresso beans.

RIGHT A Palmetto cypress stands in the Louisiana bayou, the largest wetlands in North America. Brackish in the low salt marshes near the Gulf of Mexico and flowing with fresh water upstream, the bayou teems with seafood and game birds.

RICE PUDDING

Rice pudding is a great way to use leftover rice. You may find yourself intentionally making too much rice for dinner, just so you have an excuse to make this old-fashioned custardy dessert.

SERVES 6

1 1/2 cups milk
2 tbsp. butter, melted
4 eggs, lightly beaten
1/3 cup sugar
1 tsp. vanilla
1 tsp. grated lemon peel
1/2 tsp. cinnamon
1/4 tsp. grated nutmeg
1/2 cup raisins
2 cups cooked rice

OVEN TEMPERATURE: 325°

≈ In a large bowl, mix all the ingredients together, except the rice: spices have a tendency to clump, so use a wire whisk. Stir in the rice.

≈ Pour into a buttered casserole dish (this will come right to the top of a 1 1/2-quart dish) and bake, stirring once after about 15 minutes, until the custard sets, about 1 hour. Serve warm.

RICE PUDDING

LIME MOUSSE

A light, cool dessert, that is a perfect ending for a heavy and spicy Cajun dinner. The mousse showcases the taste of lime, so fresh lime juice is strongly recommended. Make this early in the day so it has time to set. It's most spectacular served in large stemmed wine glasses.

SERVES 6–8

1 package unflavored gelatin
7 egg yolks
1 cup sugar
½ cup fresh-squeezed lime juice
1 tbsp. finely grated lime peel
7 egg whites
⅔ cup whipping cream

≈ In a small bowl, dissolve the gelatin in 3 tablespoons water. Set aside. If necessary to keep gelatin liquid, place bowl in shallow pan of hot water over very low heat.

≈ In a small bowl, beat the egg yolks until frothy, then add the sugar and beat until pale yellow. Add the lime juice and lime peel and put in top of double boiler over simmering water. Cook over low heat, stirring constantly, until mixture thickens slightly, about 10 minutes.

≈ Remove from the heat, stir in the gelatin, and set aside to cool.

≈ In a medium bowl, beat egg whites until they form soft peaks. Gradually fold the egg whites into the yolk mixture.

≈ In a medium bowl, beat the whipping cream until it forms soft peaks. Gradually fold the cream into the egg mixture until the mousse is smooth and no streaks remain.

≈ Pour into a large serving dish or individual dishes or stemware, and refrigerate at least 3 hours.

PEACH-AMARETTO ICE CREAM

What a delicious way to celebrate summer! This ice cream is made with a rich custard base and juicy, sweet, fresh peaches. Frozen ones will do in a pinch, but they are not as good. You'll need Amaretti, the light, crunchy Italian cookies made with egg whites and almond. You'll also need an ice-cream maker with a 2-quart capacity.

MAKES 2 QUARTS

1½ cups heavy cream
1½ cups whole milk
3 egg yolks
1 cup sugar
1 tsp. vanilla
4 lb. fresh peaches, peeled and stoned
1 tbsp. Amaretto liqueur or 1 tsp. almond extract
1 cup coarsely chopped Amaretti cookies

≈ In a medium saucepan, bring the cream and milk to a boil. Remove from the heat, then let cool 10 minutes.

≈ In a small bowl, beat 3 egg yolks until frothy. Add the sugar and continue beating until the mixture is pale yellow. Add a few spoonfuls of the warm cream to the eggs, to raise their temperature gently without scrambling them. Add a few more spoonfuls of cream, then whisk the egg mixture into the rest of the cream. Cook over a medium heat, just until custard thickens slightly, but do not boil. Remove from heat and stir in the vanilla. Chill at least 30 minutes or for several hours.

≈ Meanwhile, puree the peeled peaches to make 2 cups thick, chunky pulp. Add Amaretto or almond flavoring and let sit 1 hour or so.

≈ Put the cold custard and peach puree into an ice-cream maker. If your machine allows you to add ingredients easily later, wait until ice cream is partially churned before adding chopped Amaretti. Otherwise, add it now. Churn according to manufacturer's directions. Freeze until ready to serve.

LEFT   A New Orleans establishment offers mint juleps, a traditional Southern drink usually made with bourbon, sugar syrup and fresh mint.

PEACH TART WITH RASPBERRY FILLING

This tart is luscious! With fresh peaches on top and a raspberry-cream cheese filling underneath, it's almost too beautiful to eat, but too delicious not to. Be sure and use fresh raspberries and peaches. The juices from frozen fruits make the filling runny and unattractive.

SERVES 8

FILLING

2 3-oz. packages cream cheese
6 tbsp. sour cream
¼ cup sugar
1 egg yolk
1 tsp. vanilla
1 tsp. lemon juice
½ cup fresh raspberries
3 cups peeled fresh peach slices
¼ cup apricot jam

TART SHELL

1 cup flour
2 tbsp. sugar
pinch of salt
6 tbsp. chilled butter
½ tsp. grated lemon peel
2-3 tbsp. ice water

OVEN TEMPERATURE: 375°

≈ Begin by making the tart crust. Mix all the ingredients except the water, in a food processor, or in a medium bowl, using pastry cutter or a pair of sharp knives to cut in the butter until the mixture has the consistency of cornmeal. If you're using a food processor, dump the dough into a bowl at this point. Add the water, 1 tablespoon at a time, and mix gently with your hands until dough sticks together: if you do this step in a food processor, you won't be able to feel when dough is properly moistened and will probably add too much water.

≈ Gather the dough into a ball, wrap with plastic wrap, and refrigerate for at least 1 hour. Allow to sit at room temperature for another hour before rolling.

≈ Roll out the dough until it is 2-3 inches larger than 9-inch tart pan. Put the dough into the tart pan, pressing into the edges, and cut off scraps, leaving a 1-inch overhang. Pinch the overhang into a fluted crust. Line with aluminum foil. Put pie weights or beans in the crust and bake at 375° for 20 minutes. Remove pie weights and bake an additional 10 minutes. Let cool before filling.

≈ To make the filling, in a bowl, cream the cream cheese, sour cream and sugar with an electric mixer. Beat in the egg yolk, vanilla, lemon juice and raspberries, and beat until mixed. Pour into the cooled tart shell.

≈ Re-heat the oven to 375°. Arrange the peach slices on top in an attractive pinwheel design. Melt the jam and strain out any lumps, then spoon over the peaches to make a light glaze. Bake at 375° until filling is set, about 25 minutes.

PRALINE CHEESECAKE

This luscious dessert involves a number of time-consuming but not difficult steps. It's best made the night before or early in the morning it will be served. Your reward is a creamy filling with praline syrup swirled throughout and a tangy sour cream topping.

The pecans are the last things to go on the cheesecake, but should be made first to give the candy coating time to set. You will need a candy thermometer.

SERVES 12

SUGARED PECANS

3 tbsp. granulated sugar
3 tbsp. brown sugar
⅓ cup pecan halves

≈ In a small saucepan, mix the sugars and 3 tablespoons water. Bring to a boil, stirring constantly. Put the lid on and let cook 1 minute to let the sugar crystals wash down. Uncover, cook to soft ball stage, 234°, stirring constantly. Add the pecans and stir until they all are coated evenly. Remove the pecans from the syrup and place on an ungreased baking sheet to set. As soon as the coating sets, move the pecans, otherwise they will stick to the baking sheet.

GRAHAM-CRACKER CRUST

1½ cups Graham-cracker crumbs
½ cup ground pecans
3 tbsp. brown sugar
5 tbsp. butter, melted

OVEN TEMPERATURE: 350°

≈ Mix all the ingredients together: the crumbs will not form a solid mass. Press into the bottom and up sides of ungreased 9-inch springform pan: the side of the pan must be at least 2½ inches high, although the crust does not have to go all the way up. Bake 8 minutes at 350°. Let cool.

CHEESECAKE FILLING

1¼ cups granulated sugar
1½ lbs. cream cheese
8 oz. ricotta cheese
2 tsp. fresh-squeezed lemon juice
1 tsp. vanilla
3 eggs

≈ Cream the sugar and cheeses together. Add the lemon juice and vanilla, mixing at medium speed until well blended. Beat in the eggs, 1 at a time, until the mixture is smooth. Set aside.

PRALINE SYRUP

¼ cup butter
½ cup brown sugar
¼ cup heavy cream
2 tbsp. light corn syrup
¼ cup finely chopped pecans
½ tsp. vanilla

≈ In a heavy, medium saucepan, melt the butter over low heat. As soon as the butter is melted, without allowing it to brown, add the sugar, cream and corn syrup. When the sugar is dissolved and the mixture is smooth, add the pecans. Cook over medium heat, stirring constantly, for 3 minutes. Remove from heat and stir in the vanilla.

≈ Pour one-third of the filling into the crust. Drizzle one-third of the syrup over the filling in a thin stream: you don't want to form a solid layer of syrup, but create a ripple effect. Add another third of the filling and drizzle more syrup over it. Repeat with remaining filling and syrup. Bake at 350° until the top of cake is light gold, about 1 hour. Let the cake cool at room temperature, then remove outside the ring and refrigerate.

TOPPING

¾ cup sour cream
3 tbsp. powdered sugar
½ tsp. vanilla

≈ Whisk all the ingredients together. Spread over the top of the cooled cheesecake and garnish with sugared pecans.

BRUNCHES

—— ★ ——

BEIGNETS

Eat these doughnut-like treats hot with coffee, but watch for the powdered sugar that shakes onto your clothes.

MAKES ABOUT 30

½ cup water, 105-115°
1 package (¼ oz.) active dry yeast
2 tsp. sugar
¾ cup milk
½ tsp. vanilla
¼ cup unsalted butter, melted
1 egg, lightly beaten
⅓ cup sugar
1 tsp. salt
½ tsp. grated nutmeg
about 3½ cups all-purpose flour
vegetable oil for frying
powdered sugar

≈ In a small bowl, combine the warm water, yeast and 2 teaspoons sugar. Let it stand until the yeast foams and forms a head on the water, about 10 minutes. If the yeast does not foam, the water may not be hot enough to activate it, or is too hot and has killed the yeast.

≈ While the yeast is proving, combine the milk, vanilla, butter, egg, ⅓ cup sugar, salt and nutmeg. Stir in the yeast mixture. Add the flour, 1 cup at a time. After you have added 3 cups of flour, begin kneading with your hands. Add 1-2 tablespoons of flour at a time, as needed, when all the previous flour is incorporated and the dough gets sticky. Knead until smooth and elastic, 8-10 minutes.

≈ Put the dough in an oiled bowl and turn the ball over a few times until it is coated. Cover with a towel and let stand in a warm place until dough is doubled in bulk, about 1½ hours.

≈ Punch down the dough. Roll out on a lightly covered surface to ½-inch thickness. Working at a diagonal, cut the dough into 2-inch strips. Then, at the opposite diagonal, cut the strips into diamonds. Put the beignets on an ungreased cooking sheet. Knead the dough scraps into a ball, then roll out and repeat process of cutting into diamonds until you have used all the dough. Cover the beignets with towels, put in a warm place and let rise until doubled in bulk, about 1 hour.

≈ In a deep skillet or wok, heat 3 inches of oil to 365°. (Remember that when oil gets above 350° the temperature can shoot up rapidly.) Carefully put 4-5 beignets into the hot oil, making sure they don't touch each other. Fry until golden brown, turning once, 2-3 minutes a side. Remove, drain briefly, then place on paper towels and keep warm in the oven while you fry the remaining beignets. Make sure the oil returns to 365° before adding the next batch.

≈ Sprinkle the hot beignets with powdered sugar, or put sugar in a bag with a few beignets at a time and shake. Serve warm.

BREAKFAST ARTICHOKES WITH CRAB

This very rich brunch dish begins with an artichoke heart base that is filled with crab meat, topped with a poached egg, and covered with Chive-Hollandaise Sauce. If artichokes aren't available, you can substitute halved English muffins. The artichokes should be cooked ahead of time. You may also make the crab filling in advance. The technique here is an easy way to make a temperamental hollandaise sauce.

SERVES 6

2 tbsp. butter
6-8 large fresh mushrooms, coarsely chopped
1 clove garlic, minced
3 green onions, chopped
pinch of cayenne
6-8 tbsp. heavy cream
8 oz. fresh crab meat, picked over
1 green onion, chopped
1-2 tbsp. fine dry bread crumbs
salt to taste
6 artichoke hearts, cooked and trimmed
6 poached eggs

CHIVE-HOLLANDAISE SAUCE

4 egg yolks at room temperature
2 tbsp. fresh-squeezed lemon juice
1 tbsp. minced chives
1/2 tsp. salt
pinch of cayenne
3/4 cup (1 1/2 sticks) unsalted butter

≈ In a medium skillet, melt the butter. Saute the mushrooms and garlic 3–4 minutes. Add the green onions and saute 2 more minutes. Add the cayenne and 6 tablespoons cream and stir until well blended. Stir in the crab, green onion, and 1 tablespoon bread crumbs. Add additional cream or bread crumbs to moisten and bind as needed. Taste and add salt if necessary.

≈ Put all the sauce ingredients, except the butter, in a food processor but do not process yet. Melt the butter until it is bubbling but not browned. Process the yolk mixture for 3 seconds, then, while the processor is running, slowly pour in the hot butter until it is all incorporated and the sauce is pale yellow and slightly thick. The butter must be taken directly from the heat to the processor: if it is allowed to cool even slightly, sauce will not thicken.

≈ Divide the crab mixture among 6 artichokes. Top each with a poached egg. Cover with Chive-Hollandaise Sauce.

CALAS

These sweet rice cakes are deep-fried, sprinkled with powdered sugar, and served for breakfast like small pastries. They are delicious hot, and it's hard to stop with just one or two.

MAKES ABOUT 20

2 eggs
6 tbsp. sugar
2 tsp. vanilla
1/2 tsp. grated nutmeg
1/2 tsp. grated lemon peel
1/2 tsp. salt
2 tsp. baking powder
2 cups cold cooked rice
about 1 cup all-purpose flour
vegetable oil for frying
powdered sugar

≈ In a mixing bowl, combine the eggs and sugar and beat at high speed until pale yellow. Add the vanilla, nutmeg, lemon, salt, baking powder and rice, and stir until well mixed. Add enough flour, about 1 cup, to bind the ingredients.

≈ In a deep skillet or wok heat 3 inches oil to 365°. (Remember that when oil gets above 350°, the temperature can shoot up rapidly.) Drop teaspoonfuls of the batter into hot oil, but do not crowd. Fry until golden brown, turning once, about 4 minutes. Remove from the oil, drain briefly, then place on paper towels and keep warm in the oven while you fry the remaining calas. Make sure the oil returns to 365° before frying the next batch.

≈ Sift powdered sugar over the calas, or put the sugar in a bag, add a few calas at a time, and shake.

CALAS

SWEET-POTATO AND PECAN MUFFINS

These muffins are a delicious and less caloric – although not dietetic – alternative to other breakfast dishes like Beignets (page 113) and Pecan Crescent Rolls (page 117). Oat bran adds texture to the spicy dough. Bake your own sweet potato and puree the pulp, if necessary, or substitute canned pumpkin, but don't use sweet potatoes canned in heavy syrup.

I like big muffins, so I fill the cups to the brim with batter. To make more and smaller muffins, fill two-thirds full and reduce cooking time to 18–20 minutes.

MAKES 15–24

1½ cups all-purpose flour
¾ cup whole-wheat flour
6 tbsp. oat bran
1¼ tsp. baking powder
¾ tsp. baking soda
½ tsp. salt
1¼ cups brown sugar
1½ tsp. cinnamon
¾ tsp. grated nutmeg
1 tsp. grated lemon peel
6 tbsp. vegetable oil
3 eggs, lightly beaten
1½ cups sweet potato pulp
1½ cups coarsely chopped pecans

OVEN TEMPERATURE: 400°

≈ Lightly grease 2 muffin tins.

≈ In a large bowl, mix all the dry ingredients together, including the lemon peel.

≈ In a small bowl, combine the oil, eggs, ¾ cup water and sweet potato pulp. Add to dry ingredients and mix by hand, stirring only until ingredients are well blended. Stir in the pecans.

≈ Spoon the batter into the prepared muffin tins. Bake at 400° or until pick inserted in center comes out clean, 24-27 minutes.

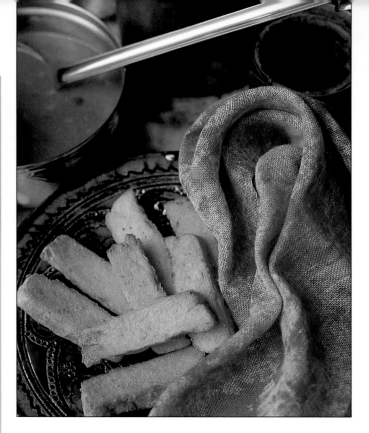

CORNMEAL MUSH

I remember eating perfectly-shaped rounds of fried mush when I was a little girl. My parents must have poured the warm mush into a tin can, let it cool, then cut off the bottom end and pushed the mush out so they could slice it in circles. This is not as pretty, but it tastes just as good formed in a loaf pan. Serve for breakfast with butter and maple syrup. Or, use the fried mush as a base, instead of rice, for gumbos and other rich-sauced dishes.

SERVES 6–8

1 tsp. salt
1 tbsp. sugar
¼ cup butter
2 cups cornmeal
vegetable oil or bacon drippings for frying

≈ In medium saucepan, bring 5 cups water to a boil. Add the salt, sugar and butter, then gradually add the cornmeal, whisking to prevent lumps. Cook over medium heat, stirring constantly. Although the water will be absorbed and the mixture thickened in just a few minutes, cook for 10 minutes longer to get rid of the raw taste.

≈ Turn into an ungreased 9½- × 5½-inch loaf pan and chill until set, at least 1 hour.

≈ In a medium skillet, heat the oil. Cut the mush in ½- to ¾-inch thick slices. Fry several slices at a time until golden brown and crispy, 6–8 minutes a side. Keep warm in the oven while frying the remaining slices.

PECAN CRESCENT ROLLS

These crescent rolls, made with a yeast dough and a sweet pecan filling, are irresistible served warm.

MAKES 24–32 ROLLS

DOUGH

1 package (¼ oz.) active dry yeast
1 tbsp. sugar
½ cup water, 105-115°
2 eggs, lightly beaten
½ cup heavy cream
⅓ granulated sugar
⅓ cup unsalted butter, melted
1 tsp. salt
about 3½ cups all-purpose flour

FILLING

½ cup unsalted butter, melted
1 cup brown sugar
4 tsp. cinnamon
1 cup pecans, finely chopped

OVEN TEMPERATURE: 375°

≈ To make dough, in a small bowl or measuring cup, combine the yeast, sugar and water. Let it stand until the yeast foams and forms a head, about 10 minutes. If the yeast does not foam, it won't rise. Make sure the water is the right temperature. If it's too cold, it won't activate the yeast, and if it's too hot, it will kill the yeast.

≈ While the yeast is proving, combine the eggs, cream, sugar, butter and salt. Stir in the yeast mixture. Add the flour, 1 cup at a time, and mix. After you have added 3 cups of flour, begin kneading with your hands. Add 1–2 tablespoons of flour at a time, as needed, when all the previous flour is incorporated and the dough gets sticky. Knead until smooth and elastic, 8–10 minutes.

≈ Put the dough in an oiled bowl and turn by hand several times until it is coated. Cover with a towel and let stand in a warm place until doubled in bulk, about 1½ hours.

≈ Meanwhile, make the filling. Make a paste of the melted butter, sugar and cinnamon, then mix in the pecans.

≈ Punch down the dough and cut in half. Roll out each half into a circle about 15 inches in diameter on a lightly floured surface. Cut each circle into 12-16 wedges, so it looks like a wheel with spokes.

≈ Spread half of filling on each circle, putting more toward the outside of the circle than in the middle. Beginning at the outside edge, roll up each wedge and turn ends in slightly so each roll resembles a crescent. Put the rolls on greased baking sheets, cover with towels, and put in warm place to rise, about 1½ hours.

≈ Bake at 375° for 12–15 minutes, watching carefully: the sugar that oozes out of the filling can burn easily, ruining the taste of the rolls.

CAJUN STRATA

Cajun Strata is the perfect way to serve traditional breakfast foods – eggs, sausage and bread – in an easy, one-dish package. Assemble it the day before and pop it in the oven one hour before eating. Serve it with fresh fruit.

SERVES 8

2 tbsp. vegetable oil
1 cup chopped onion
2 cups sliced mushrooms
2 garlic cloves, minced
½ cup chopped celery
8 cups stale bread cubes (preferably French, Italian or sourdough)
1 lb. Andouille sausage, sliced thin
¾ lb. cheddar cheese, shredded
½ cup chopped green onions
4 eggs, lightly beaten
2 cups milk
1 tbsp. Dijon-style mustard
1 tsp. salt
1 tsp. ground cumin
¼ tsp. black pepper
¼ tsp. cayenne

OVEN TEMPERATURE: 350°

≈ In a skillet, melt the butter. Saute the onion, mushrooms, garlic and celery until limp, about 5 minutes. Set aside.

≈ Lightly oil a 9-×13-inch baking dish, preferably one that can be used as a serving dish. Spread half the bread cubes in the bottom, followed by half the sausage, half the cheese, half the vegetable mixture, and all the green onions. Repeat the layers.

≈ In a small bowl, combine the eggs, milk, mustard and seasonings. Pour this mixture all over the top of strata. Cover and refrigerate overnight, allowing the bread to soak up the milk mixture.

≈ Bake, uncovered, 1 hour at 350°.

PORK GRILLADES AND GRITS

The thick, rich sauce soaks into the grits in this hearty breakfast dish to make a delicious combination. As an alternative, spoon the pork over rice and serve it for dinner. Either cook the grits following the directions on the package or as below.

SERVES 4-6

¾ tsp. salt
½ tsp. black pepper
½ tsp. cayenne
½ tsp. onion powder
½ tsp. garlic powder
½ tsp. dry mustard
¼ tsp. dried sage
1 lb. boneless pork, cut into strips
2-3 tbsp. vegetable oil
½ cup lard
½ cup all-purpose flour
½ cup chopped onion
½ cup chopped celery
½ cup chopped green pepper
1 clove garlic, minced
2 cups beef stock
2 tomatoes, seeded and chopped

GRITS

1 tsp. salt
1⅓ cups grits
3 tbsp. butter
1 egg, lightly beaten

≈ In a medium bowl, combine the seasonings. Toss with the pork strips until they are coated. Refrigerate several hours or overnight to let the meat absorb the flavors.

≈ In a medium skillet over high heat, heat the oil. Add the meat and cook until lightly browned on all sides. Remove from the heat and set aside.

≈ In a large saucepan, make a red-brown roux of lard and flour (page 15). Remove from the heat and add the onion, celery, green pepper and garlic and stir until the roux stops darkening. Return to the heat and cook until vegetables are limp, about 5 minutes.

≈ In a separate pan, heat the beef stock to boiling, then gradually add to the roux, whisking after each addition. Add the tomatoes and pork and bring to a boil, then reduce heat and simmer 45 minutes, uncovered.

≈ Meanwhile, prepare the grits in a large saucepan. Bring 4 cups water to a boil. Add the salt and gradually stir in the grits, then reduce the heat and cook, stirring constantly, until all the water is absorbed and the grits have had time to lose their raw flavor, about 10 minutes. Stir in the butter and egg.

≈ Just before serving taste and adjust seasoning of the pork mixture. Ladle over the grits and serve.

SAUCES AND
DRESSINGS

— ★ —

COCKTAIL SAUCE

TARTAR SAUCE

This tangy sauce uses bottled mayonnaise as a base, but if you are comfortable using raw eggs, begin with your own mayonnaise recipe and omit the olive oil and sour cream.

MAKES ABOUT 1½ CUPS

2 tbsp. olive oil
1 cup mayonnaise
2 tbsp. sour cream
1 tbsp. fresh-squeezed lemon juice
¼ cup chopped sweet pickles
1 tbsp. chopped capers
2 tbsp. finely chopped green onion
1 clove garlic, minced
½ tsp. salt
¼ tsp. black pepper

≈ In a small bowl, whisk the olive oil into mayonnaise, until it is incorporated. Whisk in the sour cream and then the remaining ingredients. Chill at least 2 hours to let the flavors blend.

COCKTAIL SAUCE

Prepare this tangy red sauce, with the sharp bite of horse-radish, several hours ahead and refrigerate so the flavors blend. Serve with Boiled Shrimp (page 65) or crab, or Deep-Fried Oysters (page 22).

MAKES ABOUT 1¼ CUPS

½ cup ketchup
½ cup bottled chili sauce
2 tbsp. prepared horseradish
1 tbsp. Dijon-style mustard
1 tbsp. fresh-squeezed lemon juice
1 tbsp. white wine vinegar
1 tbsp. Worcestershire sauce
2 green onions, minced
¼ tsp. salt
¼ tsp. black pepper
few drops of Tabasco sauce, to taste

≈ In a medium bowl, combine all ingredients and whisk together. Refrigerate until ready to serve.

MUSTARD SAUCE

MUSTARD SAUCE

Here is a delicious and tangy alternative to red cocktail sauces to use as a dip for seafood.

MAKES ABOUT 1¼ CUPS

1 cup sour cream
3 tbsp. Dijon-style mustard
2 tbsp. mayonnaise
1 tbsp. chopped fresh dill or 1 tsp. dry dill weed
fresh-ground black pepper

≈ In a small bowl, whisk all the ingredients together. Chill for several hours to allow the flavors to blend.

VINAGRETTE

This flavorful salad dressing is excellent on green salads and pasta salads. If you prefer, substitute whatever fresh herbs are available.

MAKES ABOUT ½ CUP

½ cup olive oil
2 tbsp. white wine vinegar
2 tsp. fresh-squeezed lemon juice
1 garlic clove, finely minced
2 tsp. Dijon-style mustard
1 green onion, finely chopped
¼ tsp. salt
⅛ tsp. black pepper
2 tsp. finely chopped fresh basil
1 tsp. finely chopped fresh oregano

≈ In a jar, combine all the ingredients and whisk or shake well. Refrigerate for several hours to let the flavors blend.

VINAGRETTE

BUTTER SAUCE FOR FISH

This rich, creamy sauce is delicious with Crab-Stuffed Fish (page 62) or Grilled Shark (pages 60–61).

MAKES 4–6 SERVINGS

1 green onion, finely chopped
2 tbsp. dry white wine
2 tbsp. white wine vinegar
¼ cup butter
¼ cup heavy cream
salt
white pepper

≈ In a small saucepan, simmer the onion, wine and vinegar until the liquid is reduced to 1 tablespoon. Over very low heat, whisk in the butter, 1 tablespoon at a time. Whisk in the cream until smooth. Warm, but don't let sauce bubble. Season with salt and pepper to taste.

VARIATION:

≈ Add 1 tablespoon chopped fresh dill at the beginning, before the reduction. Add 1 more tablespoon chopped fresh dill with the salt and pepper. This variation works particularly well with the Grilled Shark recipe (pages 60–61).

RÉMOULADE SAUCE

Traditionally this sauce is mixed with cold cooked shrimp and served over lettuce with various garnishes such as tomatoes and olives, but it can also be used as a seafood dip. With recent health concerns about use of uncooked eggs, I based this sauce on bottled mayonnaise. If you're comfortable using raw eggs, begin with your own home-made mayonnaise recipe, and omit the olive oil and sour cream.

MAKES ABOUT 1 CUP

1 tbsp. olive oil
½ cup mayonnaise
2 tbsp. sour cream
1 hard-boiled egg, shelled and finely chopped
1 tbsp. capers, drained and chopped
1 clove garlic, squeezed through garlic press
1 tbsp. finely chopped fresh parsley
2 green onions, minced
2 tbsp. ketchup
1 tsp. lemon juice
1 tbsp. Creole mustard
½ tsp. prepared horseradish
¼ tsp. cayenne
¼ tsp. salt
few drops of Tabasco sauce

≈ In a medium bowl, whisk the olive oil into the mayonnaise until it is all absorbed. Add the remaining ingredients and whisk until smooth. Check the seasoning and adjust, then chill for several hours or overnight to let flavors blend.

INDEX